Digital Business Models and Environmental Action

Adam Jabłoński · Marek Jabłoński

Digital Business Models and Environmental Action

Harnessing Technological Revolution to Address Climate Change

palgrave
macmillan

Adam Jabłoński
WSB MERITO University in Poznan
Poznań, Poland

Marek Jabłoński
WSB MERITO University in Poznan
Poznań, Poland

ISBN 978-3-032-15297-8 ISBN 978-3-032-15298-5 (eBook)
https://doi.org/10.1007/978-3-032-15298-5

This Palgrave Macmillan imprint is published by the registered company Springer Nature Switzerland AG
The registered company address is: Gewerbestrasse 11, 6330 Cham, Switzerland

This book is dedicated to Professor Henryk Arctowski and Professor Antoni Bolesław Dobrowolski, Polish polar explorers and members of the famous Belgica scientific and research expedition, considered the world's first climate scientists

Preface

The aim of the monograph is to present core strategic problems related to the technological revolution in business, the economy and society related to the digital, energy and climate revolution through the new business models of companies.[1]

The problem creates opportunities for shaping new, positively changing business models using the potential of the ongoing dynamic technological, digital, energy and climate revolution of socio-economic ecosystems.

The book concerns specialist knowledge in the field of management and quality sciences and climate sciences and technical science theory. This idea will be presented in this monograph.

The monograph is in line with the Nobel prizes in economics awarded in 2025. This year, Joel Mokyr (Northwestern University, Tel Aviv University), Philippe Aghion (Collège de France, INSEAD, London School of Economics) and Peter Howitt (Brown University) were honored. The prizes were awarded 'for explaining innovation-driven

[1] Adam Jabłoński, a co-author of the monograph, is a member of a research team in a Scientific Project financed as a result of a foreign competition: European Climate, Infrastructure and Environment Executive Agency (CINEA) CINEA.C—Green research and innovation C.1—Horizon Europe Climate, GRANT AGREEMENT, Project 101056933—Climateurope2. This project refers to the fact that the reality of climate change is strongly felt in unprecedented extreme climate conditions, among many other impacts that have significant consequences for current socio-economic systems.

economic growth.' Philippe Aghion and Peter Howitt received the prize for their research into innovation-driven economic growth, in particular for developing assumptions for growth theory through the mechanism of creative destruction. Joel Mokyr, on the other hand, was honored for his analysis of the historical and institutional conditions for the development of innovation. He indicated that sustainable technological progress requires not only skills in how something works (prescriptive knowledge), but also understanding why it works (propositional knowledge). The model of economic growth through creative destruction developed by Philippe Aghion and Peter Howitt is based on the assumption that new ideas supersede outdated solutions. Innovation is not just an addition; it is a mechanism for structural change. In this context, the authors of this monograph wished to point out that technological progress and innovations based on creative destruction in the field of creating digital business models can affect the neutralization of negative climate effects and even positive climate change, which is currently a challenge for our generation. Creative destruction, which is the nucleus of innovative change, stimulates progress, which, using a dynamic balance, promotes the creation of creative solutions in the field of climate services and the search for solutions dedicated to the search for breakthrough technologies that halt adverse climate change threatening the current *status quo* in relation to economic, political and social issues. In order to illustrate the complexity of the issue presented in the monograph, the components that are chapters within the scope of the authors' original concept of digital business models and environmental action and harnessing the technological revolution to solve the problem of climate change have been presented graphically in Fig. 1.

The presented model identified a closed cycle of implementation of the principles of digital business models, environmental action and harnessing the technological revolution to solve the problem of climate change. This proposed model is described in detail in this scientific monograph. The monograph indicates the theoretical and practical determinants of digital business models, environmental action and harnessing the technological revolution to solve the problem of climate change. The book is preceded by this preface. Chapter one broadly describes the place and role of the technological revolution in the relevant literature. It indicates the principles of technological revolution in the relevant literature against the background of the issues of climate change and the theory

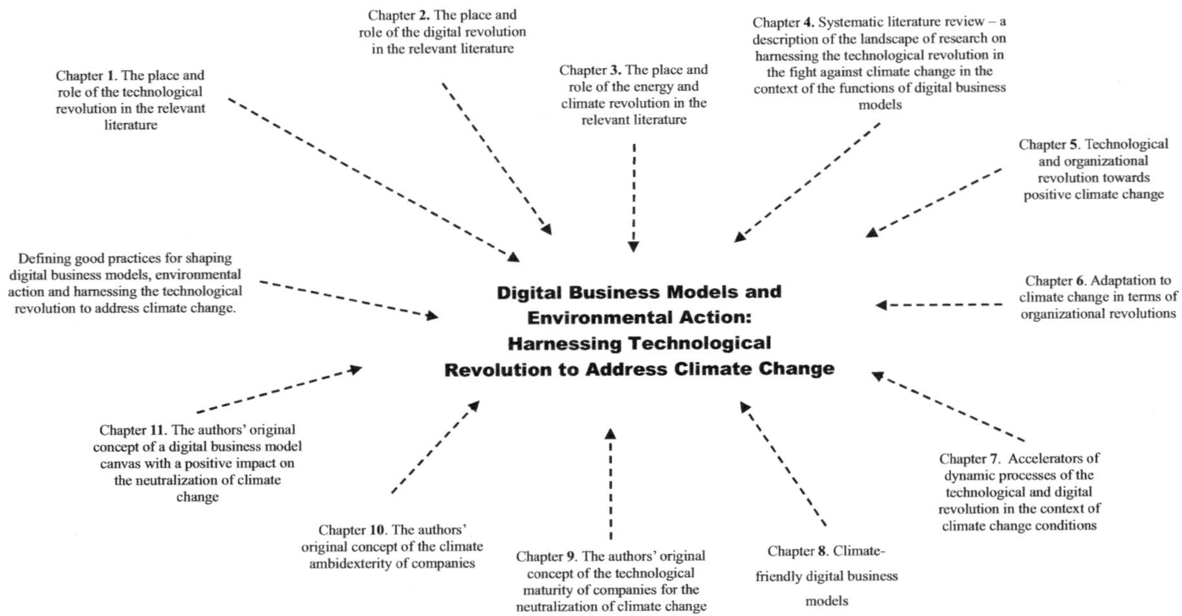

Fig. 1 Concept of digital business models, environmental action and harnessing the technological revolution to address climate change. (*Source* Own study)

of intelligent technical systems in the dynamics of technological development of the economy and society. Chapter two refers to the place and role of the digital revolution in the relevant literature. It describes, among others, digital business models and cyber-physical systems and their impact on environmental actions and processes of the digital transformation of companies and their impact on optimizing the effect on the natural environment. The place and role of the energy and climate revolution in the relevant literature are described in chapter three, which focuses on various structures of energy mixes as a platform for the energy revolution in climate adaptation changes and the principles of energy and climate engineering in shaping climate responsibility. In turn, chapter four discusses the systematic literature review—a description of the landscape of research on harnessing the technological revolution in the fight against climate change in the context of the functions of digital business models. Chapter five is devoted to the important issue of the technological and organizational revolution aimed at positive climate change. It describes, among others, the architecture of dynamic climate systems in climate change adaptation processes and the solutions of the Industry 4.0 and 5.0 concepts as intelligent production focused on ecological and climate issues. Chapter six details a number of solutions that define the principles of adaptation to climate change in terms of organizational revolutions. This chapter contains practical solutions and scientific proposals for managers to improve and develop the strategic management of climate knowledge and climate responsibility, as well as strategic management of regions and cities oriented towards climate responsibility. Chapter seven presents the accelerators of dynamic processes of the technological and digital revolution in the context of the determinants of climate change; particular reference is made to the factors determining the impact of the technological revolution on the success of companies—the principles of implementing innovative green solutions—creative destruction and, among others, artificial intelligence and solutions for smart geolocation and the application of Artificial Geospatial Intelligence (GeoAI) in climate adaptation processes. Chapter eight describes climate-friendly digital business models. Three further chapters, i.e., chapters nine, ten and eleven, present the authors' original concepts. Chapter nine presents the authors' original concept of the technological maturity of companies for the neutralization of climate change. Chapter ten presents the authors' original concept of the climate ambidexterity of companies, and chapter eleven describes the authors' original concept of a digital business model canvas that has a positive impact on the neutralization of climate change. The last chapter, chapter twelve, outlines the definition of good practices for shaping digital business models, environmental action and harnessing the technological revolution to address climate change. The monograph ends with the conclusion.

Poznań, Poland

Adam Jabłoński
Marek Jabłoński

Competing Interests The authors have no competing interests to declare that are relevant to the content of this manuscript.

Contents

About the Authors

Adam Jabłoński is Full Professor at WSB MERITO University in Poznan, Poland.

He is also Vice-President of the Board of the reputable management consulting company 'OTTIMA plus' Sp. z o.o. (Ltd.), Katowice, and President of the 'Southern Railway Cluster' Association, Katowice, which supports development in railway transport and innovation transfer, as well as cooperation with European railway clusters (a member of the European Railway Clusters Initiative). He holds a postdoctoral degree from the University of Łódź (Department of Management), Poland, specializing in Management Science (Business Models, Strategic Management). Having worked as a management consultant since 1997, his experience and expertise has grown through his cooperation with a number of leading companies in Poland and abroad. He is the author of a variety of studies and business analyses on the Strategic Performance Management Concept, Value-Based Management and the design of Digital Social Business Models. He has also written or co-authored several monographs and over 100 scientific articles in the field of management, published both in Poland and in abroad. His scientific interests are focused on the issues of modern and efficient strategic management methods and new approaches to the design of a strategic group of key performance indicators and the principles of company value building sustainable strategy. He attempts to integrate the assumptions of strategic management with a configuration approach to shaping business models, as well as monitoring and evaluating their effectiveness. He also explores various features of modern strategic measurement systems and the operationalization of strategy and business models oriented towards achieving high performance. Currently, he is also a member of the scientific boards of national and international journals and a scientific reviewer for different entities. He is the author of numerous monographs, publications, articles and scientific concepts published in Poland and independently in prominent publishing houses, including Taylor & Francis Group—Routledge, Palgrave Macmillan, Springer Nature, Nova Publishers and IGI Global, and the author of many scientific articles published in world-renowned journals. He has been a featured speaker at numerous scientific and industry conferences and congresses, as well as the initiator of a number of scientific and business ventures. He also conducts extensive research on the design and implementation of business models that positively impact the climate, taking into account the principles of Digital and Climate Transformation supported by Artificial Intelligence solutions. He is a member of a research team operating in accordance with Evidence-Based Management (EBM) standards. He specializes in the search for, analysis of and implementation of scientific and applied solutions based on scientific evidence. His research focuses on the development of new scientific solutions, systematic literature reviews, assessment of the quality of scientific research and the transfer of knowledge and technology to improve management practice and managerial decisions. He is a member of the scientific and research project 'Confraternity of Scientific Evidence-Based Management', where he conducts research on the application of the Evidence-Based Management concept in the discipline of management science and quality. He strives to mainstream this scientific concept in scientific research and business management. He is a co-author of scientific articles promoting and exploring the potential of this concept in relation to science and business practice, and actively seeks scientific and practical opportunities to disseminate knowledge about the concept of evidence-based management. He is a member of a research team in a Scientific Project chosen in an international competition: European Climate, Infrastructure and Environment Executive Agency (CINEA) CINEA.C—Green research and innovation C.1—Horizon Europe Climate, GRANT AGREEMENT, Project 101056933—Climateurope2. This project addresses the fact that the reality of climate change is felt in extreme climatic conditions, among many other effects that have significant consequences for the functioning of socio-economic systems.

Marek Jabłoński is Associate Professor at WSB MERITO University in Poznań, Poland.

Marek Jabłoński is Associate Professor, PhD (Polish habilitation) in Economic Sciences, specializing in Management Science, namely the disciplines of Value-Based Management and the Performance Management concept, the business models of companies at an early stage of development, startup expansion and the green strategies of enterprises. He is Professor at WSB MERITO University and President of the reputable management consulting company OTTIMA plus Ltd. in Katowice (the Silesia region of southern Poland).

He is also Vice-President of the Southern Railway Cluster, which supports development in railway transport and innovation transfer, as well as cooperation with European railway clusters (a member of the European Railway Clusters Initiative). He has been working as a management consultant since 1999, and his experience and expertise has grown through his contact with a number of leading companies in Poland and abroad. He is the author of a variety of studies and business analyses on enterprise value, risk management, the balanced scorecard, business models, startup strategy and entrepreneurships. He has also written and co-written over 10 monographs and over 200 scientific articles in the field of management. Marek Jabłoński's scientific interests focus on the value-based management concept and creating value of companies at an early stage of development, as well as climate-changing aspects and their influence on industry and the business models of companies. He is also an expert in safety management in railway enterprises. He is the author of numerous monographs, publications, articles and scientific concepts published in Poland and independently in prominent publishing houses, including Taylor & Francis Group—Routledge, Palgrave Macmillan, Springer Nature, Nova Publishers and IGI Global, and the author of a number of scientific articles published in world-renowned journals. He has been a featured speaker at many scientific and industry conferences and congresses, and the initiator of many scientific and business ventures. His research also focuses on the assessment of the investment attractiveness of companies based on business model criteria. He conducts extensive research on the design and implementation of business models that positively impact the climate, taking into account the principles of

Digital and Climate Transformation supported by Artificial Intelligence solutions. He is a member of a research team operating in accordance with Evidence-Based Management (EBM) standards. He specializes in the search, analysis and implementation of scientific and applied solutions based on scientific evidence. His research focuses on the development of new scientific solutions, systematic literature reviews, assessment of the quality of scientific research and the transfer of knowledge and technology to improve management practice and managerial decisions. He is the initiator and founder of the scientific and research project 'Confraternity of Scientific Evidence-Based Management', where he conducts research on the application of the Evidence-Based Management concept in the discipline of management science and quality. He strives to mainstream this scientific concept in scientific research and business management. He is a co-author of scientific articles promoting and exploring the potential of this concept in relation to science and business practice, and actively seeks scientific and practical opportunities to disseminate knowledge about the concept of evidence-based management.

List of Figures

List of Tables

CHAPTER 1

Introduction

Abstract The main objective of the scientific discussion in this monograph is to present core strategic problems pertaining to the technological revolution in business, the economy and society related to the digital, energy and climate revolution through new business models of companies.

Keywords Business models · Digital revolution · Technological revolution · Harnessing of technology · Digital business models

The main objective of the scientific discussion in this monograph is to present core strategic problems pertaining to the technological revolution in business, the economy and society related to the digital, energy and climate revolution through new business models of companies.

As part of the scientific goal, it is crucial to determine the scientific problem and identify the cognitive gap. This cognitive gap is an identifiable set of factors for digital business models, environmental action and harnessing the technological revolution to address climate change. Such a defined cognitive scope should lead to the emergence of the development of digital business models, environmental action and harnessing the technological revolution to address climate change. This concept should be in

A. Jabłoński and M. Jabłoński, *Digital Business Models and Environmental Action*,
https://doi.org/10.1007/978-3-032-15298-5_1

line with the current conditions of the European approach to the development of digital business models, environmental action and harnessing the technological revolution to address climate change. Theoretical and practical factors should emerge against the background of this concept which determine changes in the perception of technological progress, the search for projects requiring funding and which have an impact on reversing the adverse impact of climate change on the functioning of regions, cities and companies, as well as through the prism of threats such as the loss of the quality of life, prosperity and security of human existence.

The authors understand the concept of digital business models, environmental action and harnessing the technological revolution to address climate change as an interdisciplinary set of approaches to business management by incorporating such components in the configuration of business models that support activities for the pro-climate operation of companies on the market. This should create a 'snowball' effect for all companies that wish to remain on the market and set new technological and organizational trends against the background of new conditions for doing business and creating assumptions for incorporation into political and social processes.

This is part of a broad approach to shaping the concept of digital business models and actions to reverse climate change and the use of technology through revolution to solve the problem of climate change against the background of sciences such as economics and finance, climate sciences, management and quality sciences. Such a presentation of the issue requires the definition of new assumptions of the theory of digital business models, environmental action and harnessing the technological revolution to address climate change.

As part of the theoretical assumptions related to the solution of a defined scientific problem pertaining to the concept of digital business models, environmental action and harnessing the technological revolution to address climate change, an analysis was carried out to embed this problem in the theory of management sciences. In order to correctly diagnose the phenomenon occurring in science, it is crucial to use reliable analyses and the interpretation thereof in scientific discussions. For this purpose, however, it is necessary to combine the determinants of understanding the concept of digital business models, environmental action and harnessing the technological revolution to address climate change.

Table 1.1 Sequence of activities within the research method of the concept of digital business models, environmental action and harnessing the technological revolution to solve the problem of climate change

No	*Sequence of activities of the research method of the mechanisms of digital business models, environmental action and harnessing the technological revolution to solve the problem of climate change*
	Collecting relevant literature on the subject of the issues of digital business models, environmental action and harnessing the technological revolution to address climate change
	Identifying the components of digital business models, environmental action and harnessing the technological revolution to address climate change
	Defining the scope of influence of various factors on the development of digital business models, environmental action and harnessing the technological revolution to address climate change
	Defining the features characterizing the specificity of creating digital business models, environmental action and harnessing the technological revolution to address climate change
	Analyzing the contextual conditions of the market in relation to the development of digital business models, environmental action and harnessing the technological revolution to address climate change and their practical implementation
	Defining good practices for shaping digital business models, environmental action and harnessing the technological revolution to address climate change
	Developing analyses, the resulting synthesis, conclusions and recommendations for building digital business models, environmental action and harnessing the technological revolution to address climate change
	Determining the theoretical determinants of creating digital business models, environmental action and harnessing the technological revolution to address climate change
	Identifying new directions of the development of digital business models, environmental action and harnessing the technological revolution to address climate change in theoretical and practical terms

Source Own study

The research method pertaining to the concept of digital business models, environmental action and harnessing the technological revolution to address climate change adopted a sequence of actions, which is presented in Table 1.1.

The diagram of the process of the research procedure in empirical sciences and the process of diagnostic procedure in psychology developed by Spendel (2005), interpreted for the purpose of conducting advanced research into digital business models, environmental action and harnessing the technological revolution to address climate change, is presented below (Table 1.2).

The crucial conditions necessary for maintaining the correct implementation of the research strategy have been maintained. This enabled the creation of both a research framework and the conducting of extensive theoretical and practical research. The study is cognitive–evaluating and based on multidimensional scientific inference. The book covers the assumptions of creating a new theory related to the presentation of core strategic problems related to the technological revolution in business, the economy and society associated with the digital, energy and climate revolution through new business models of companies and elements covering practical solutions.

The subject of the scientific discussion includes scientific and practical digressions on components forming a coherent system of mechanisms of digital business models, environmental action and harnessing the technological revolution to address climate change.

Cognitive objectives include:

1. Identifying factors responsible for shaping digital business models, environmental action and harnessing the technological revolution to address climate change.
2. Determining the relationships between the different elements in shaping digital business models, environmental action and harnessing the technological revolution to address climate change.
3. Assessing the impact of digital business models, environmental action and harnessing the technological revolution to address climate change on the effectiveness and efficiency of organizational management.
4. Assessing the relationship between technological transformation, digital transformation, electricity transformation and climate transformation through the concept of business models.
5. Searching for technological changes that will be conducive to the reversal of adverse climate phenomena already implemented at the level of companies, but also through the awareness of employees and their individual behavior in everyday life.

Thus, the following research questions were posed:

Table 1.2 Diagram of the process of the research procedure in empirical sciences and the process of diagnostic procedure in psychology developed by Spendel, Z. (2005), interpreted for the purpose of conducting advanced research into digital business models, environmental action and harnessing the technological revolution to address climate change

Scientific research—classical	*Scientific study on climate responsibility in business models*	*Diagnostic procedure—classical*		*Diagnostic procedure—climate responsibility in business models*
Recognizing and verbalizing the research problem concerning the relationship between selected phenomena, formulating a preliminary hypothesis and (possibly) showing the circumstances of the problem	The recognition and verbalization of the research problem results from the current needs of the manager and he/she is the generator of the research problem. The research problem is a reflection of a real managerial problem in a business run by a manager He/she can independently conduct the research process with regard to the research problem posed and/or use the help of a professional researcher. The circumstances of addressing a given research problem are the specific, actual and current context of the organization in a given socio-economic ecosystem in which the company exists	**Conceptualization**	Preliminary identification and assessment of the problem and justification for addressing it—this usually means finding some irregularities	A problem is recognized and verbalized as part of a diagnostic procedure only by a manager who needs to solve a given diagnostic problem. The manager, noticing some problems that occur in the organization, looks for effective and efficient ways to solve them

(continued)

Table 1.2 (continued)

Scientific research—classical	*Scientific study on climate responsibility in business models*	*Diagnostic procedure—classical*		*Diagnostic procedure—climate responsibility in business models*
Positioning the problem and hypothesis in a theoretical context, defining the assumptions and formulating research subhypotheses in terms of relationships between the separated variables	Positioning the problem and hypothesis in a theoretical context, defining the assumptions and formulating research subhypotheses in terms of relationships between the separated variables	**Concretization**	Formulation of detailed questions and diagnostic hypotheses on the genesis and pathomechanism of the identified abnormality	The manager develops a problem that bothers him/her in detail, which he/she must solve. For this purpose, it generates research questions or hypotheses
Determination of the criteria of empirical applicability and quantitative recognition for observational terms occurring in subhypotheses	The manager and/or the researcher assisting him/her develops an execution framework in terms of the algorithm of solving a given problem. He/she can use artificial intelligence solutions here	**Operationalization**	Planning (or selecting an appropriate model) of the diagnostic procedure and the selection of suitable (i.e., relevant to the hypotheses) diagnostic methods	The manager prepares a list of specific steps along with the proposed diagnostic methods
Selection of models for collecting and organizing experience compared with the content of empirical implications of hypotheses and models of data analysis. Application of selected research and statistical models of selected research and statistical models	The manager and/or the researcher assisting him/her makes a constructive comparison of the principles of experience management in the organization and the results of evidence research, comparing the results of resource management in a given organization with the research problem to be solved	**Confrontation**	Collection of data by means of selected methods and analysis of results in terms of their compliance with diagnostic hypotheses	The manager aggregates the obtained results and compares them with a problem in the area of diagnostic procedures, verifying them through previous decision-making processes in the same or a similar area of business

Scientific research—classical	*Scientific study on climate responsibility in business models*	*Diagnostic procedure—classical*		*Diagnostic procedure—climate responsibility in business models*
Formulation of conclusions on the veracity of the tested hypotheses, as well as the indication of the acceptable reference range of the obtained research results to: 1) assumptions and research hypotheses, 2) the possibility of formulating further problems, possibly proposing theoretical and methodological postulates, revising the current paradigm, and 3) taking practical actions on that basis	The manager and/or researcher assisting him/her will develop a set of goals to achieve research results. It takes into account, in the form of possible micro-corrections, information, data and knowledge from other sources supporting the decision-making processes	**Application**	Formulation of the diagnosis (in the form of conclusions, opinions, rulings, etc.) and postulates regarding corrective, therapeutic conduct and cooperation with other specialists and institutions	The manager interprets, diagnoses and synthesizes the results obtained as a result of the procedure, correcting them, if necessary, for other resulting sources that may correct potential errors in the decision-making diagnostic process

Source Own study based on Spendel (2005)

1. Can companies with top managers focused on reversing climate change, through their actions, foster processes that reverse climate change?
2. Can modern theories, technologies, concepts, solutions, methods and models serve to neutralize the risk of climate change-based phenomena?
3. Are individual actions against the background of global strategies of large corporations at all noticeable in the wider climate context?
4. Does it make sense to engage in the processes of climate change neutralization in the absence of threats to military, economic, social and migration security and the speed of technological change, which has been staggering in recent years?
5. Can a human being influence climate change by supporting his or her conscious actions in this regard?
6. What technologies and technological and organizational solutions can support the processes of reversing the trend of climate change, which affects weather anomalies and changes in the structure of the functioning of the earth as a planet?

In addition, in connection with pursuing the purpose of the monograph, two research hypotheses were put forward and subsequently verified:

Hypothesis 1: The technological revolution strengthens the fight against climate change through environmental action.
Hypothesis 2: The functions of digital business models influence the fight against climate change.

It is important to prove these hypotheses because of the importance of the scientific problem, as well as the real risks arising from dynamic climate change in natural and socio-economic ecosystems.

Methodological objectives include:

1. Indicating the configuration of factors that shape the principles of digital business models, environmental action and harnessing the technological revolution to address climate change.
2. Developing strategic recommendations for the development of principles for digital business models, environmental action and harnessing the technological revolution to address climate change.

3. Developing the authors' original concept of the technological maturity of companies for the neutralization of climate change.
4. Developing the authors' original concept of the climate ambidexterity of companies.

Utilitarian objectives include:

1. Developing the authors' original methodology for shaping digital business models, environmental action and harnessing the technological revolution to address climate change—developing the authors' original concept of a digital business model with a positive impact on climate change neutralization.
2. Developing a set of management, technical and operational factors that have the greatest impact on creating the principles of digital business models, environmental action and harnessing the technological revolution to address climate change.

Due to the multidimensionality and holistic nature of the functioning of companies, the topic of the scientific discussion requires one to address issues related to the theory of management and quality sciences, economics and finance, climate sciences and the theory of technical sciences.

This book is based on the following limitations:

1. There has been no extensive research into digital business models, environmental action and harnessing the technological revolution to address climate change. No significant experience in this regard exists.
2. There are no solutions to reverse climate change at the company level.
3. There is no development of dedicated assumptions for formulating strategies of companies oriented towards the naturalization of climate change such as the model of climate ambidexterity proposed in the monograph.
4. The proposed solutions are experimental solutions supported by research into the relevant literature and observations of companies focused on climate change, taking into account the applied modern technologies conducive to these processes and requiring

their appropriate adaptation to the specific conditions of modern business.
5. A limitation is the still relatively low awareness among top managers in relation to profit goals and positive influences on climate change for the benefit of the human race in general.

Time relevance, the importance of issues and the contribution to science of issues related to the mechanisms of digital business models, environmental action and harnessing the technological revolution to address climate change.

By writing this monograph, the authors wished to bring added value to the identification, conceptualization and operationalization of the implementation of the principles of digital business models, environmental action and harnessing the technological revolution to address climate change. The proposed research issue is generally not presented with such a broad approach in the relevant literature. The value of the creative contribution is related to the presentation of a comprehensive approach to the principles for digital business models, environmental action and harnessing the technological revolution to address climate change. The authors would like to draw attention to the need to develop a new theory of building and implementing the principles of digital business models, environmental action and harnessing the technological revolution to address climate change, as well as to indicate utilitarian solutions that provide guidance for managers of various types of companies interested in developing the principles of digital business models, environmental action and harnessing the technological revolution to address climate change. Figure 1.1 shows the relationship between the processes of digital transformation of companies and climate transformation, which lead to the emergence of a technological revolution, as a result of which new inclusive business models are created in response to technological progress and changes in social and business ecosystems.

This presentation of the joint and synergistic implementation of the assumptions of climate and digital transformations opens up a whole spectrum of new business and societal opportunities towards the creation of climate-smart digital values that can be transformed into new and innovative climate-friendly digital business models.

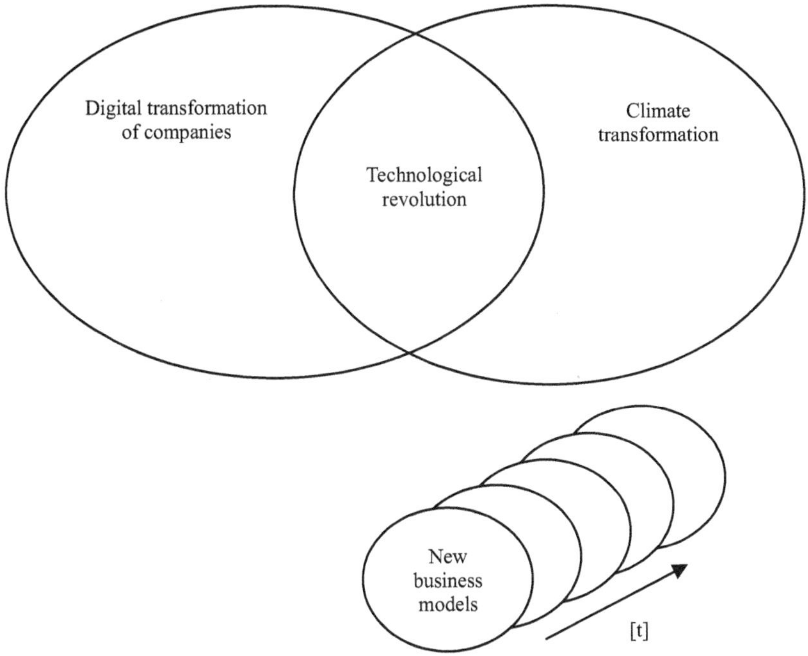

Fig. 1.1 Inclusive new business models emerging against the background of changes resulting from the digital transformation of companies and the climate transformation (*Source* Own study)

References

Spendel Z. (2005). *Methodology of psychological research as a form of historical consciousness*. University of Silesia Press.

CHAPTER 2

The Place and Role of the Technological Revolution in the Relevant Literature

Abstract The aim of this chapter is to present place and role of the technological revolution in the relevant literature. The technological revolution should be treated as a period of rapid breakthroughs and changes in technology that radically affect people's way of life, the functioning of the economy and the development of society. The technological revolution in digital business models and environmental action, and in particular in the fight against climate change, is a great challenge for modern economies. Business management in the context of digital transformation faces huge challenges, where the current paradigms, solutions and theoretical foundations of decision-making are undergoing significant changes. Technology is essentially part of every step of business operations. Each process, operation or transmission of information is based on the assumptions of technological changes in terms of the manner of execution and reception of the processes carried out. Therefore, management without technological support is futile and fits into the old paradigms, which are already largely outdated.

Keywords Technological revolution · Digital business models · Digital transformation · Climate change

A. Jabłoński and M. Jabłoński, *Digital Business Models and Environmental Action*,
https://doi.org/10.1007/978-3-032-15298-5_2

2.1 Introduction

The technological revolution should be treated as a period of rapid breakthroughs and changes in technology that radically affect people's way of life, the functioning of the economy and the development of society. The technological revolution in digital business models and environmental action, and in particular in the fight against climate change, is a great challenge for modern economies. Business management in the context of digital transformation faces huge challenges, where the current paradigms, solutions and theoretical foundations of decision-making are undergoing significant changes. Technology is essentially part of every step of business operations. Each process, operation or transmission of information is based on the assumptions of technological changes in terms of the manner of execution and reception of the processes carried out. Therefore, management without technological support is futile and fits into the old paradigms, which are already largely outdated. Transferring archaic knowledge to academic textbooks and proving that it is relevant show's creators who do not accept the fact that most management paradigms need to be redefined in a bad light. The factors influencing these needs are revolutionary changes in the processes of designing business models based on digital platforms, technology fusions of key providers of innovative solutions, the implementation of socio-technical systems based on new principles taking into account the factors of technological progress and the inclusion of engineers, as those who, with today's technological approach to the functioning of digital business models, better understand the interdisciplinarity of these processes and bring a significant amount of new knowledge and added value to the creation of new theories, concepts, models and practical solutions. This is proven by the modern literature: articles and monographs, but also grey literature, where creative solutions violating the current rules that fit into the concept of 'game changers' are presented. Specific technological solutions stimulate the emergence of new business models based on the improvement of processes supported by modern digital technologies. For example, Industry 5.0 has the ability to surpass the technology-oriented performance of Industry 4.0 and accelerate the achievement of the SDGs, such as prioritizing human needs, ensuring socio-environmental sustainability and increasing resilience. Digital twins and simulation technologies improve production, evaluate products and operations and anticipate any potential negative effects. Thanks to digital twin technology, everything that exists in the physical world will eventually be duplicated in the digital sphere (Yang et al., 2024). These tools of the digital economy stimulate completely different assumptions of designing digital business models, different conditions for creating strategies, different conditions for strategic thinking, new principles of designing business models, different principles of creating revenues, including monetization, and other principles of cost structure. Thus, most current solutions in the field of understanding knowledge of management processes are changing and new paradigms are being created requiring further knowledge and the search for new research spaces in the field of building theories in the discipline of management and quality sciences. Therefore, the evolutionary driver that directs companies' knowledge and attention in specific directions means that companies need multiple sources of Big Data to be resilient and dynamic (Pedota, 2023). Modern systems, in their logic, provide a good balance between complexity and comprehensiveness. The five dimensions of the proposed framework are the physical entity (PE), the digital model (DM), the physical-to-digital (P2D) updating method, the digital-to-physical (D2P) updating method and continual optimization (OPT) across all dimensions. A physical unit refers to a physical equivalent (a component, a machine or a machine system) which is a twin. The P2D dimension converts data generated from the following sources:

1. The physical unit, from the physical state to the state of the digital model. The digital model optimizes some aspects of the digital state and generates valuable insights that can be influenced to bring about an appropriate change in the physical state. The D2P dimension forces these observations through human or machine intervention.
2. Optimization has an impact on all dimensions of the digital twin, serving to optimize the acquisition of data from the physical unit, the estimation of parameters and state and the interaction of people with the digital twin through the D2P dimension. OPT can be further divided into offline and online elements (van Eyk & Heyns, 2025). The technological revolution is also developing widely under the influence of changes in the awareness of the world's citizens in the context of climate change hazards and the resulting climatic anomalies and dysfunctions threatening the life processes of the inhabitants of the earth and animals, plants and other

adverse weather phenomena in the existing ecosystem. Technological and environmental advances have been negatively linked to the ecological footprint. Thus, more environmental technologies reduce non-renewable energy consumption, and environmental technologies provide less energy consumption and therefore a lower ecological footprint (Aziz et al., 2024). The technological revolution of modern business also stems from the issue of the use of energy from renewable sources, which consists of three core stages, namely energy generation, transmission and distribution. Energy storage and trade are secondary but necessary steps in renewable energy production, as renewable energy production faces numerous challenges in terms of efficiency and reliability (Pandey et al., 2023, pp. 171–188). Since the world is not equal in terms of the standard of technological progress, sustainable solutions must be sought that give other regions of the world a chance of success. In resource-rich countries, supporting the development of digitalization, characterized by an increased number of fixed broadband subscriptions and digital infrastructure, correlates with more efficient resource management. On the other hand, the impact of digital progress on resource management practices in resource-poor countries appears to be less pronounced, which indicates potential challenges in using digital technologies to manage resources in these contexts (Manu & Asongu, 2025). Thus, it can be observed that the technological revolution changes the rules of the global economy and affects not only global processes, but also local conditions for the functioning of companies. Today's digital revolution has changed the course of global development, and now we live in the era of the information society in which nuclear energy, digital electronics, space technology and many others are widely used. The progress of the world in all spheres of management is developing exponentially. In the new world, information takes first place, which is of paramount importance in modern realities (Kartsan & Mavrin, 2023, pp. 116–119). The technological revolution affects many areas of life and business and is divided into numerous different categories. In terms of macro- and microeconomics, its division may include the digital revolution from two perspectives, namely Fintech and Innovation and Entrepreneurship (Kutan, 2024). From the perspective of human relationships, the digital revolution has a lot to say. Fostering productive network relationships with organizations inside and outside the value chain enhances the competitiveness of businesses. The ongoing digital platform revolution is facilitating these online relationships (Falcao Peruchi et al., 2022, pp. 344–363). Thus, the technological revolution affects many, if not all, spheres of business and life. The new rules for managing and creating business models must be based on revolutionary solutions. Technological progress is even exponential in the context of contemporary technological determinants. In such conditions, not all companies are able to adapt to new realities and can be displaced by new entities focused on maximizing the use of innovations that violate the current market rules. In J. Schumpeter's approach (Schumpeter, 1942) it was called creative destruction and now has a significant application. Figure 2.1 presents contemporary transformations in the processes of creative destruction in the creation of technological business models.

The graph presents assumptions for contemporary changes in the processes of creative destruction aimed at the creation of technological business models. The diagram is complex, covering what happens between people using technological solutions initiated by technological revolutions, financial technologies and innovation and entrepreneurship. The digital revolution is based on the assumptions of creative destruction, which offers opportunities to create new business models that take into account new management rules resulting from technological progress. Factors generating revolutionary solutions are extracted from the external and internal environment.

2.2 Technological Revolution in the Relevant Literature Against the Background of Climate Change

Observing the present reality closely, it is impossible not to notice the exponential impact of an avalanche of changes of different nature in every area of human functioning. This de facto destabilizes the existence of socio-economic ecosystems strongly shaped by technology. This is accompanied, on the one hand, by the creation of new products, services, solutions and concepts and, on the other hand, by the total destruction of the current world as seen through the eyes of the recent past.

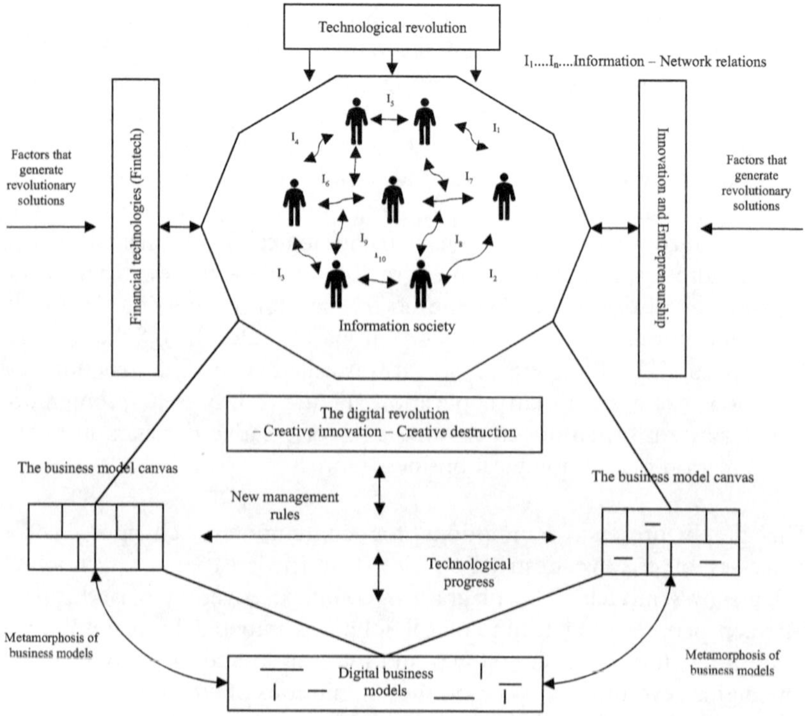

Fig. 2.1 Contemporary transformations in the processes of creative destruction aimed at the creation of technological business models (*Source* Own study)

Hence, the fundamental issue is the question—and the attempt to provide an answer—of whether today's world is in the stage of revolution or technological evolution, especially in the area of climate change.

The concept and issue of climate change eludes human intelligence with its vastness and scope. Being a phenomenon of implied importance, characterized by practically unlimited spatial, logistical and temporal range with simultaneous unevenness of occurrence, it is an example of a so-called hyperobject (Morton, 2013). The issue of climate change is considered in almost all social, technical, economic, ecological and political fields, as well as in the context of military conflicts. The main causes of adverse climate change generating weather anomalies, including violent storms, floods and hurricanes, intense heat, inadequate cold during the seasons where such states arouse surprise, intense rainfall, but also changes of a geological or hydrological nature regarding forest management, are recognized by most experts as those resulting from the excessive exploitation of land resources for the development of industry or predatory policy of exploitation of deposits. The modern technological revolution should be focused on neutralizing the risks associated with the adverse impact of industry on climate change and be innovative enough to influence change effectively. For many years, a number of technological solutions have been oriented towards supporting the pro-ecological activities of politicians and managers who care about the natural environment. Figure 2.2 shows the relationships between selected variables with an impact on climate change.

They worry about what land they will leave to the next generations so that they can fully enjoy its beauty and landscapes and that the citizens of the world will live safely and not have to migrate for climate reasons to more climate-attractive areas of the world. The role of technological innovation in reducing pollution and wider negative impacts is motivated by increased global emissions (Khurshid et al., 2021, p. 1). Technology can play a role in solving environmental problems, although structural action is also needed if we are to create a future sustainable society (Cramer & Zegveld, 1991, p. 451). The source of the search for structural solutions is solutions resulting from progress in the digital economy. The global changes of recent years indicate that the boundary

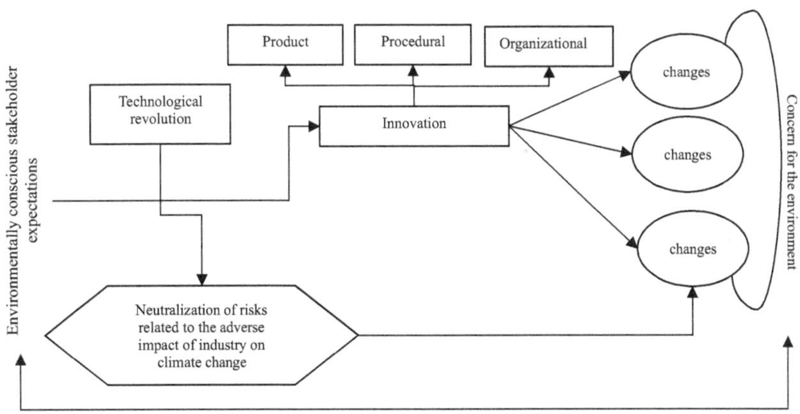

Fig. 2.2 Relationships between selected variables with an impact on climate change (*Source* Own study)

between the physical and digital worlds is becoming increasingly blurred. An increased number of sectors of society are moving online and digital technologies are increasingly affecting industrial, agricultural, scientific, medical, educational and other processes. Digitalization technologies have a particular impact on the evolution of traditional views on environmental protection methods. The further development of digital technologies will at least reduce hydrocarbon consumption and greenhouse gas emissions and help mitigate the effects of e-waste. The use of digital environmental technologies as part of global environmental monitoring, improving the safety of industrial enterprises, in agriculture, as well as improving the comfort of living in the urban environment, is quite promising. Environmental policy discussions are increasingly focused on issues related to technological change. This is partly because the environmental consequences of social activity often depend on the pace and direction of technological change, and partly because environmental policy interventions can create constraints and incentives that have a significant impact on the path of technological progress (Jaffe et al., 2001, p. 1). Such an embedded scientific problem triggers the need to identify solutions aimed at technological progress, but focused on climate change, minimizing adverse impact on the natural environment, social and ecological impact, improving the quality of life of citizens and balancing business goals for the needs of social balance and acceptance of a modern approach to business and industry creation, while taking into account social needs. It also affects the high demands for air cleanliness, land use, green spaces, the elimination of the 'concrete urban sprawl' and other consequences of mismanaging the development of industry, cities and villages without respect for the environment, both locally and globally. The leading direction of the technological revolution in the context of climate change and attempts to neutralize the adverse impact of human civilization on its dysfunctions is the design of predictive systems and services that capture anomalies, instability and discontinuous phenomena affecting unexpected weather changes and climate changes such as the melting of glaciers, changes in the functioning of groundwater and the creation of flood phenomena and excessive heat. It should be noted here that the technological revolution aimed at this neutralization and limiting and reversing the adverse impact of humans on climate change refers, among others, to the dynamic response to the temperature drop and shrinking of the upper atmosphere. This also applies to climate phenomena such as increasing tropopause levels and less oxygen in the air. Attention should also be paid to the elements aimed at nights warming faster than days, as well as more coal from fossil fuels in the air. It is important to know that winters are warming faster than summers and that there is more heat returning to the earth. In addition, there are more fossil fuels embedded in coral skeletons and dynamic ocean heating. Figure 2.3 shows governments' responses to phenomena caused by climate change.

This creates new services for monitoring these phenomena with information and warning functions. These underlie the creation of scenarios to defend against the effects of such phenomena and the search for strategies to halt these dangerous trends in the medium and long term. The AI revolution offers the tools with the greatest potential to bring about a radical transformation of interaction to understand the disputes between the public, the scientific community and the political community. These interactions should aim to strengthen human efforts to better understand the greatest mystery of all: the origin and function of the world and our place in it, i.e., the tasks of science itself (Bianchini et al., 2022, p. 1). This is particularly true of the issue of climate change, when the analysis of changes, their simulations and predictions serve to determine new scenarios of behavior in the macro, meso and micro spheres. AI foresight strengthens the ability to influence the future development of different sectors of the economy. The technological revolution in this

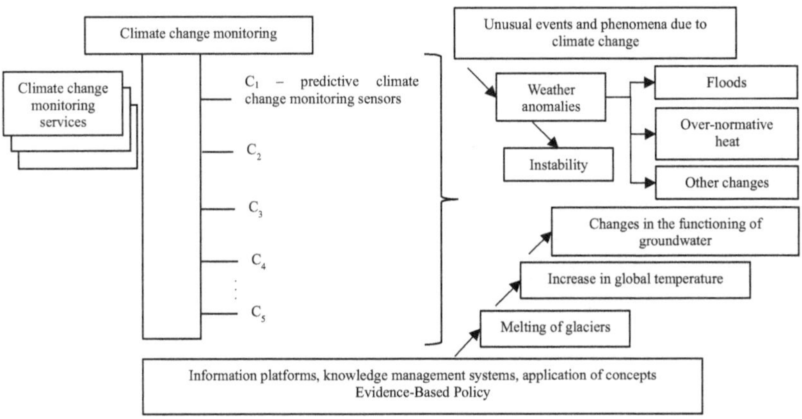

Fig. 2.3 Governments' response to phenomena caused by climate change (*Source* Own study)

area is highly visible and manifests itself in various proposals for solutions for their implementation and adaptation to dynamic changes. Artificial intelligence and other advanced technologies have permeated numerous aspects of the supply chain of many industries and services over the years. The creation of a machine equipped with intelligence requires, above all, the free exchange of information between it and man, as well as between it and the environment in which it is to function (Hołyński, 1979, p. 76). One such example is the food sector. As a result, AI solutions in this area are perfectly equipped to develop new models for predicting future threats to food safety caused by climate change (Karanth et al., 2023, p. 1). There are many such solutions and they are developing dynamically in the context of various conditions of searching for the ability to create monetizing business formulas in the form of startups. Figure 2.4 shows the drivers of startups supporting the development of climate change monitoring systems.

The creation of startups is stimulated by changes in social ecosystems, which open new space for the creation of business solutions.

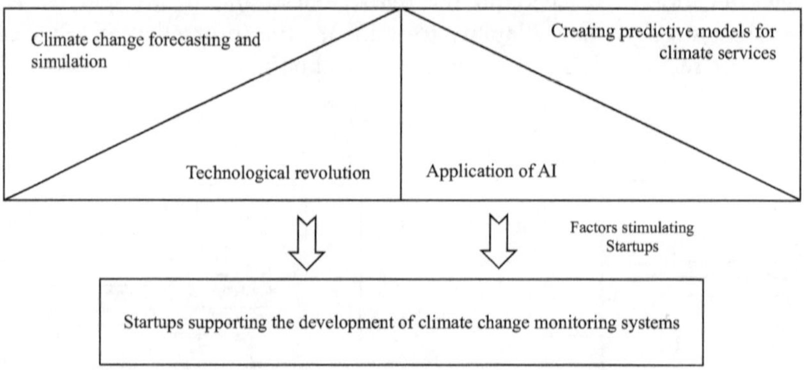

Fig. 2.4 Factors stimulating the emergence of startups supporting the development of climate change monitoring systems (*Source* Own study)

2.3 The Theory of Intelligent Technical Systems in the Dynamics of Technological Development of the Economy and Society

The dynamics of technological development in modern industry result from the adopted boundary conditions, which are embedded in the theory of intelligent technical systems that are based on the concept of a System of Systems. A system is a set of interrelated elements. Thus, a system is an entity that consists of at least two elements and a relationship that occurs between each of its elements and at least one other element in the set. Each element of the system is connected to each other, either directly or indirectly. Furthermore, no subset of elements is unrelated to any other subset. Intelligent technical systems can be understood as systems using modern technologies, sensors, algorithms and software to automatically monitor, analyze and control processes in an adaptive and optimal way. A static (one-state) system is one in which no events occur. A dynamic (multi-state) system is one in which events occur, whose state changes over time. A homeostatic system is a static system whose elements and environment are dynamic. Thus, a homeostatic system is one that retains its state in a changing environment by means of internal adjustments (Ackoff, 1971). Figure 2.5 shows the examples of interdependencies between intelligent technical systems. The issues of the roles of intelligence carriers supporting the achievement of the expected functions of the system were highlighted. The sum of systems and their functions supported by intelligence carriers shapes an intelligent system of systems.

Technological and industrial systems based on automation, robotization, artificial intelligence and technical diagnostics determine the mechanisms of the dynamically progressing technological revolution of the modern world. The stream of overlapping crises in recent years has triggered an avalanche of changes in various areas of human existence, almost completely changing the polarization of the functioning of economies, business and society. The rapid growth of solutions has even flooded social and economic ecosystems, causing a shock reaction among older groups, among others. The impact of the avalanche of changes has been both top-down and bottom-up: top-down through these social, health, military, economic and climate crises and bottom-up through changes in human behavior at the level of, among others, the labor market and the sphere of private human life. This approach is supported by the

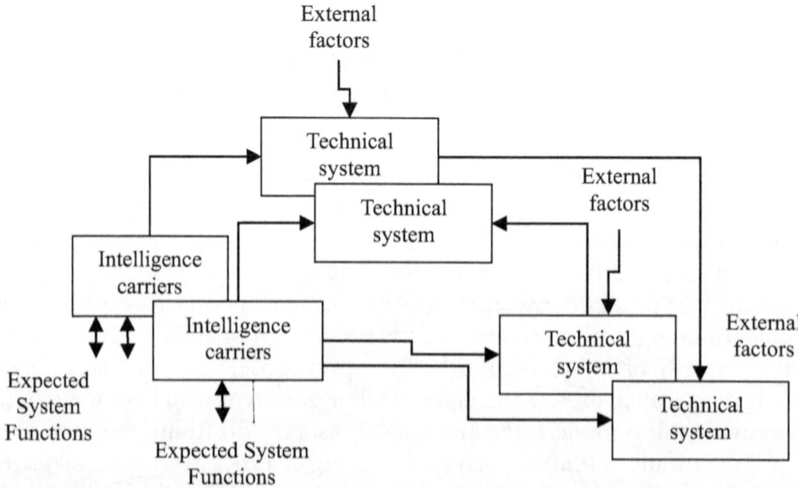

Fig. 2.5 Examples of dependencies between intelligent technical systems (*Source* Own study)

use of a strategy called fusion strategy, where the model of operation is based on the creation of technology fusion—cooperation, where the individual parties to the contract contribute 'technological engines' at different levels of technological maturity, such as source codes for the creation of databases, artificial intelligence algorithms, robotization and diagnostics schemes, creating one common project on that basis that gives multidimensional value to all participants in this merger. CarPlay is a system designed by Apple that integrates the iPhone with the car's multimedia system. It allows for the use of selected applications and features of the phone, such as navigation, phone calls, messages, music, podcasts and others, directly on the car screen. Thanks to CarPlay, drivers can safely and comfortably use the phone's functions while driving, without taking their eyes off the road. Based on this concept, the business creation model is bottom-up: players combine their potential into one attractive product, which creates opportunities to deliver new value to customers and thus creates the possibility of technological cooperation based on technologies defined at the appropriate level of maturity, creating new value, as shown in Fig. 2.6.

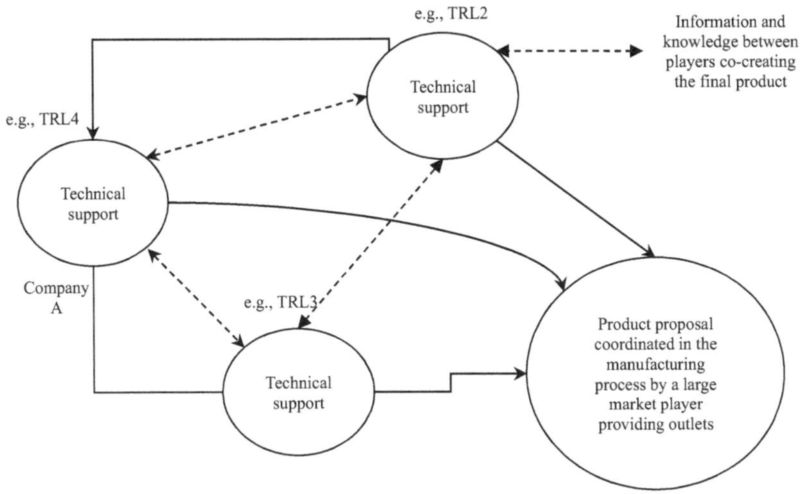

Fig. 2.6 The assumptions of Fusion Strategy in the context of the technological revolution (*Source* Own study based on V. Govindarajan, V. Venkatraman, Fusion Strategy, How Real-Time Data And AI Will Power the Industrial Future, Harvard Business Review Press, Boston, Massachusetts [2024, pp. 75–79])

The presented approach explains the new model of bottom-up strategic value creation. In the first step, it is necessary to identify the technological potential and the maturity levels of individual partners of the project in order to develop a new value proposition from them. It can be based either on the form of a partnership project between peers or on obtaining support by a large player who plays the role of a consortium leader. Such a solution will support partners not only in technological but also marketing terms.

In order to be able to create and implement breakthrough and revolutionary technological solutions, multidimensional and achievable total social cohesion is needed as a criterion for the creation of innovative climate technologies. A properly aggregated relationship between society XE Society and the creators of modern technologies, and supporting innovative institutions supporting these processes is then required.

Figure 2.7 presents a triad of total social cohesion as a criterion for the development of innovative climate technologies.

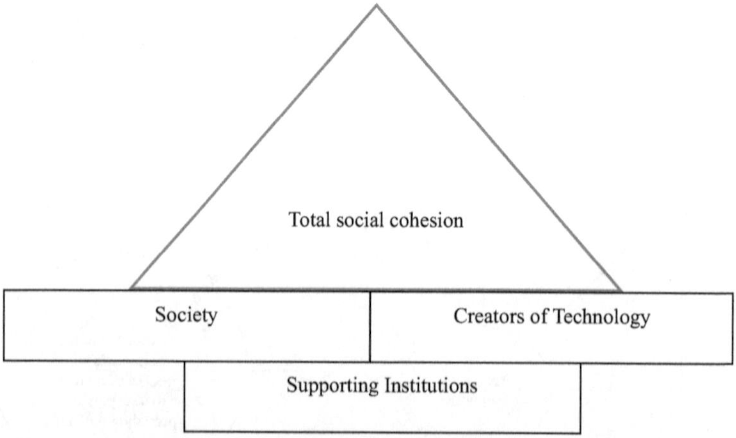

Fig. 2.7 The triad of total social cohesion as a criterion for the creation of innovative climate technologies (*Source* Own study)

Total social cohesion in the environment of the functioning of social technical systems requires that both technical and social issues constitute one common ecosystem in which new solutions and new value propositions for customers are created. This ecosystem must be complementary to the needs of different stakeholder groups. The key drivers of such an ecosystem are emerging innovations. Factors stimulating the creation of new space include people, technology, products, equipment, information, distribution channels, partnerships, foundations and brands (Johnson, 2010, p. 40). However, one needs to be able to notice the signs of a warming world in the context of observing glaciers, snow cover, land temperature, air humidity, air temperature near the Earth (troposphere), the degree of shifting of tree boundaries towards the poles and upwards, the temperature above the oceans, sea surface temperature, the ocean level, ice sheets and the heat content of the ocean. These factors belong to traditional resources, but digital resources such as cloud computing, Big Data and scientific evidence data, digital networks, artificial intelligence, automation, robotization and diagnostics solutions, digital platforms and other solutions that constitute the ecosystems of digital society and business cannot be ignored. Figure 2.8 shows the place and role of the value generated by the socio-business ecosystem in the context of climate goals.

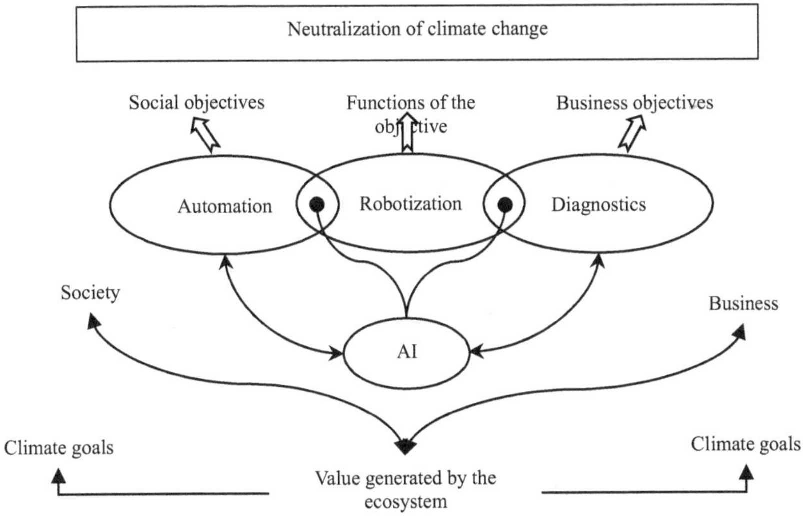

Fig. 2.8 The place and role of the value generated by the socio-business ecosystem in the context of climate goals (*Source* Own study)

Climate change can only be neutralized by designing a new approach to life and business that, based on automation, robotization and diagnostics supported by artificial intelligence, supports climate goals through a partnership of all societal stakeholders in a sustainable way.

The development of technology economies in shaping climate change may generate new levels of competitive advantage in technology markets. This is primarily important because the vast majority of economic solutions are currently based on innovative, modern technologies. The key to their proper application is the level of their technological readiness.

Technology readiness levels (TRL) are used to define the level of technological advancement and help compare the state of technological advancement. The pioneer of the TRL methodology was the US agency NASA in the 1980s.

The use of this methodology helps determine the technological maturity of the product from the conceptual phase to the finished solution, applicable in practice. It is therefore possible to compare the technological levels in completely different fields. The European Commission bases its assessment of projects on the TRL methodology. The assumption is to determine how close or far a given product or service is from implementation. The Technology Readiness Level is assessed on the basis of a scale from 1 to 9. Level 1 defines the conceptual phase of a solution and Level 9 should be understood as a full technology readiness level enabling the application of the technology in real-world conditions. The use of this scale will also make it possible to assess what validation work has already been carried out and what needs to be done in order to launch the product on the market in the future.

Level 1—the lowest level of readiness. It is the starting point for further research and development of the idea. At this level, the initial assumptions and concept of future technology are created.

Level 2—the formulation of the technological concept. This level is the starting point for the process of creating innovation. The problem is defined and the assumptions are planned.

Level 3—reached when experimental evidence confirming the accepted thesis is carried out. Analytical and laboratory tests are performed at this stage.

Level 4—reached when the first attempts are made to develop and test a prototype in laboratory conditions resulting from a combination of earlier stages of technology.

Level 5—the level of technological validation of the developed prototype in a near-real-world environment.

Level 6—the biggest technological leap from level 5. The developed technology is presented and tested in real conditions. At this stage, one can already talk about the likelihood of creating a final product in reality that will fulfill its tasks.

Level 7—this is the moment of demonstration of the developed prototype in the operating environment. The test makes it possible to make corrections and further develop the technology.

Level 8—technological readiness, which is the final stage of technological development. At this stage, the evidence process pertaining to the operation of the technology in reality has been completed. The tests are completed with a positive result. At this stage, the final version of the technical, training and service documentation is developed.

Level 9—the highest technology readiness level. The developed technology works and the resulting product is ready for production and sale on an industrial scale.

The intersection of artificial intelligence and robotics has undoubtedly ushered in a new era in automation. This transformative collaboration is recognized as an increase in intelligent machines endowed with the ability to learn, adapt and perform complex tasks autonomously. Machine learning algorithms, which are the cognitive backbone of robotic frameworks, are central to this philosophical movement. These algorithms involve robots to analyze infinite data sets, observe complex projects and dynamically optimize forms in real time (Nishar, 2023, p. 1). Artificial intelligence technology in industrial automation control systems is becoming the core technology for the future development of the industry. Due to the limitations of the current technology level and application mode, AI technology still has many limitations in industrial automation control systems, which requires experts and scientists in the relevant fields to use AI technology wisely according to the development features and real needs of industrial automation technology to further improve the overall performance of the industrial automation control system (Li, 2021). Industrial AI is developed in five areas, namely infrastructure, data, algorithms, decision-making and objectives (Silva Peres et al., 2020). Thinking machines or mechanical social robots for the climate? This is one of the most important questions in the context of the technological revolution in the area of climate change.

The quantum revolution can also be used in the processes of positive adaptation of climate change.

Quantum technologies refer to a set of advanced technological solutions based on the principles of quantum physics. Quantum theory includes the following branches of theoretical physics: non-relativistic and quasi-relativistic quantum mechanics, quantum multi-body theory, quantum thermodynamics, quantum optics, quantum computing, various variants of quantum field theory (including the standard model of elementary particles) and quantum cosmology (Jacyna-Onyszkiewicz, 2015). Quantum solutions provide a strong platform for climate challenges and problems and are therefore a huge opportunity to reverse adverse climate polarization. By providing and utilizing enormous computing power, quantum technology can significantly improve and strengthen modeling processes for difficult-to-control climate change. Quantum technologies can create incredible breakthroughs, not least technological ones, in the digital, energy and climate transformation. The incredible ability of quantum technology to process vast amounts of information and data much faster than before opens a wide path to surprising breakthroughs in climate science. The potential of quantum technology and its solutions can make a significant contribution to a new shape and image of sustainability and sustainable business. Quantum intellectual space for green climate technologies is clearly being created. For example, quantum information techniques are being developed on experimental and theoretical levels. They are situated between classical information techniques, computer engineering, ICT and on the other hand quantum mechanics and its limitations. The development of Quantum IT, despite the considerable distance from the technical maturity of this discipline as a whole, also initiates research in the post-quantum direction (Romaniuk, 2023). In the area of artificial intelligence, quantum computers are used in machine learning. In the area of cybersecurity, quantum computers in quantum cryptography are used to encrypt and transmit data. In relation to the use of quantum computers in Big Data sets, the Grover algorithm is used to search large volumes of data. It helps find a specific element in unstructured databases faster, and to solve computationally difficult problems faster at different levels of complexity. Figure 2.9 shows a scheme for the use of quantum technologies in climate change monitoring and adaptation processes.

From this perspective, quantum technologies and thus quantum computers offer a huge opportunity to solve different problems and perform different types of simulations much faster, which can contribute to better management of natural resources, improve different types of energy and develop more sustainable technologies, including climate technologies. Quantum theories are also the basis of modern cryptography used in the creation of climate governance mechanisms.

2.4 Conclusions

The technological revolution in the broad dimension of the world economy accelerates progressive market and social changes. This is primarily the result of the overlapping of different types of technology supported by other areas of science and economic practice. It is impossible to stop but it is possible to properly steer it towards what is positive and expected by society. The social impact on technological development is fundamental. Intelligent technological systems should generate different types of values, including climate values. A noticeable trend of creating new and positive technological changes towards climate protection and neutralizing the negative direct and indirect impacts on the climate can be observed.

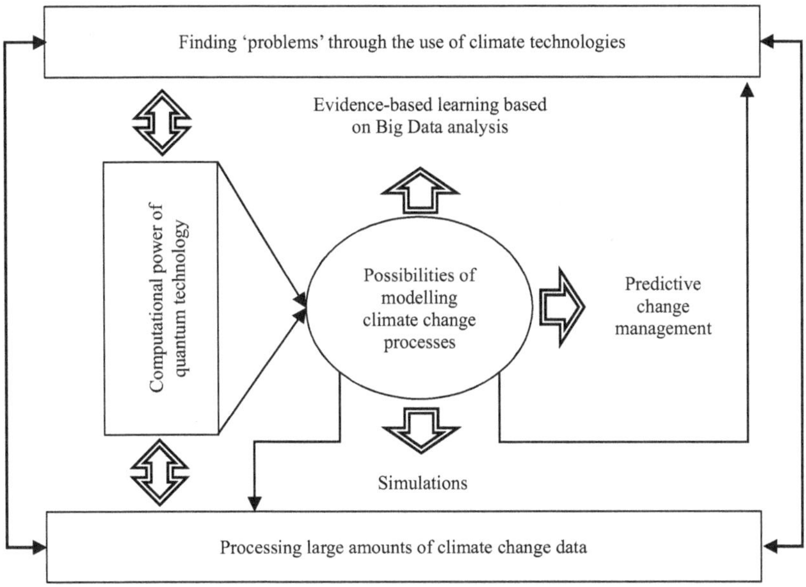

Fig. 2.9 Diagram of the use of quantum technologies in climate change monitoring and adaptation processes (*Source* Own study)

References

Ackoff, R. L. (1971). Towards a system of systems concepts. *Management Science, 17*(11), 661–671.

Aziz, G., Strielkowski, W., Sarwar, S., & Kumar Tiwari, A. (2024). Implications of circular economy, digitalization and technological innovation to achieve sustainable environmental goal: Pre- and post-vision 2030. *Heliyon, 10*, Article e30978.

Bianchini, S., Müller, M., & Pelletier, P. (2022). Artificial intelligence in science: An emerging general method. *Research Policy, 51*(10), Article 104604.

Cramer, J., & Zegveld, W. C. L. (1991). *The future role of technology in environmental management* (p. 451). Futures Butterworth-Heinemann Ltd.

Falcao Peruchi, D., Augusto de Jesus Pacheco, D., Villa Todeschini, B., & Schwengber ten Caten, C. (2022). Moving towards digital platforms revolution? Antecedents, determinants and conceptual framework for offline B2B networks. *Journal of Business Research, 142* (2022) 344–363.

Hołyński, M. (1979). *Sztuczna inteligencja [Artificial intelligence]* (p. 76). Wiedza Powszechna.

Jacyna-Onyszkiewicz, Z. (2015). Fundamentalna Zasada Teorii Kwantowej, Konferencja ChFPN Nauka – Etyka – Wiara [Fundamental Principle of Quantum Theory, ChFPN Science – Ethics – Faith Conference]. *Rydzyna, 4–7*(06), 2015.

Jaffe, A. B., Newell, R. G., & Stavins, R. N. (2001). *Technological Change and the Environment* (Discussion Paper 00–47REV, p. 1).

Johnson, M. W. (2010). *Seizing the white space, Business model innovation for growth and renewal* (p. 40). Harvard Business Press.

Karanth, S., Benefo, E. O., Patra, D., & Pradhan, K. A. (2023). Importance of artificial intelligence in evaluating climate change and food, safety risk. *Journal of Agriculture and Food Research, 11*, 1.

Kartsan, P., & Mavrin, S. (2023). The digital revolution of the transportation industry. *Transportation Research Procedia, 68*, 116–119.

Khurshid, A., RaRauf, A., Calin, A. C., Qayyum, S., Hussain Mian, A., Qayyum, S., & Fatima, T. (2021). Technological innovations for environmental protection: role of intellectual property rights in the carbon mitigation efforts. Evidence from western and southern Europe. *International Journal of Environmental Science and Technology*, Published online, 1.

Kutan, A. M. (2024). Digital revolution, blockchain technologies and central bank digital currencies: Implications for Asian economic cooperation. *Asia and the Global Economy, 4*, Article 100080.

Li, Q. (2021). *Application of Artificial Intelligence in Industrial Automation Control System, ICAESEE 2020 IOP Conf. Series: Earth and Environmental Science* (Vol. 647, p. 012043). IOP Publishing. https://doi.org/10.1088/1755-1315/647/1/012043

Manu, E. l K., & Asongu, S. A. (2025). The impact of environmental policy, technological innovations, and digitalisation: Does context matter in natural resource management in Sub-Sahara Africa? *The Extractive Industries and Society, 22*, 101608.

Morton, T. (2013). *Hyperobjects: Philosophy and ecology after the end of the world*. University of Minnesota Press.

Nishar, S. (2023). Artificial intelligence in automation and robotics: Transforming industries and enhancing efficiency, 2023 ijcspub | Volume 13, Issue 4, | ISSN: 2250–1770 of invention. *Research Policy, 51*, 1.

Pandey, V., Sircar, A., Bist, N., Solanki, K., & Yadav, K. (2023). Accelerating the renewable energy sector through Industry 4.0: Optimization opportunities in the digital revolution. *International Journal of Innovation Studies, 7*, 171–188.

Pedota, M. (2023). Big data and dynamic capabilities in the digital revolution: The hidden role of source variety. *Research Policy, 52*, Article 104812.

Romaniuk, R. (2023). Kwantowa Europa, kwantowa Polska, Przegląd Telekomunikacyjny Rocznik, *XCVI Wiadomości Telekomunikacyjne Rocznik XCII*, nr 2/2023. https://doi.org/10.15199/59.2023.2.2

Schumpeter, J. (1942). *Capitalism, socialism and democracy*. Harper & Brothers Publishers New fork and London.

Silva Peres, R., Colombo, A. W. (Member, Ieee), Jia , X., Lee, J. (Fellow, IEEE) Barata, J., & Sun, K. (Member, IEEE). (2020). Industrial Artificial Intelligence in Industry 4.0 Systematic Review, Challenges and Outlook, IEEE Access. https://doi.org/10.1109/ACCESS.2020.3042874, *Digital Object Identifier*.

van Eyk, L., & Heyns, P. S. (2025). A framework to define, design and construct digital twins in the mining Industry. *Computers & Industrial Engineering, 200*, Article 110805.

Yang, T., Razzaq, L., & Atika Qazi, F. (2024). Redefining fan manufacturing: Unveiling industry 5.0's human-centric evolution and digital twin revolution. *Heliyon, 10*, 33551.

CHAPTER 3

The Place and Role of the Digital Revolution in the Relevant Literature

Abstract The aim of this chapter is to present place and role of the digital revolution in the relevant literature. The digital revolution covers most areas of human existence and continues to spread. However, it must be technologically, economically and socially justified. Its embedment in business, the economy and society should be based on the logic of benefits and the creation of new values. Only then will it be able to generate streams of various types of opportunities to improve the quality of life of humanity as a whole. The digital revolution can be seen as a process of transition from various analog to digital technologies, in which relevant information, communication and data processing become digital, leading to highly significant changes in the economy, society and daily human existence. The digital revolution should be based on core scientific paradigms so that its results are positive and can be fully controlled by society. Only under the conditions of scientific knowledge will all its applications be able to be monitored and verified for the benefit of the general public as opposed to selected social groups. In this regard, it is important to implement and develop it in such a way that there are no social exclusions resulting, for example, from the lack of access to digital solutions. This also applies to the sphere of digitalization for the creation of positive climate change.

A. Jabłoński and M. Jabłoński, *Digital Business Models and Environmental Action*,
https://doi.org/10.1007/978-3-032-15298-5_3

Keywords Digital Revolution · Digital technologies · Digital solutions · Climate change

3.1 Introduction

The digital revolution covers most areas of human existence and continues to spread. However, it must be technologically, economically and socially justified. Its embedment in business, the economy and society should be based on the logic of benefits and the creation of new values. Only then will it be able to generate streams of various types of opportunities to improve the quality of life of humanity as a whole. The digital revolution can be seen as a process of transition from various analog to digital technologies, in which relevant information, communication and data processing become digital, leading to highly significant changes in the economy, society and daily human existence. The digital revolution should be based on core scientific paradigms so that its results are positive and can be fully controlled by society. Only under the conditions of scientific knowledge will all its applications be able to be monitored and verified for the benefit of the general public as opposed to selected social groups. In this regard, it is important to implement and develop it in such a way that there are no social exclusions resulting, for example, from the lack of access to digital solutions. This also applies to the sphere of digitalization for the creation of positive climate change.

3.2 Assumptions for Digital Game Changer Solutions and Their Impact on Shaping Climate-Changing Business Models

In recent years, management theorists and practitioners have been searching not only for solutions that, as it were in the old nomenclature, are conducive to building a competitive advantage, but are rather a game changer solution, i.e., they change the rules of the game in the sector in a broader sense. Most often, these include digital platforms with such attractive functionalities that are considered fashionable and broaden the spectrum of people's quality of life. Product–service systems (PSSs) often serve this purpose when companies, contrary to the traditional offer of a pure product, offer a combination of them—a joint consideration of products and services. Such an assumption therefore consists in the fact that the sale primarily concerns the service provided by the product, which changes consumer perceptions and the traditional business model of the company, and also results in consumers preferring services that have a positive impact on the environment. A good example of a product and service platform is Volvo Connect, which is a suite of combined B2B services and technologies offered by Volvo that allows the company's customers to access a range of services and dashboards through the Volvo On Call app, including real-time traffic information, remote startup, climate control and the ability to locate and lock a vehicle (Ritala & Jovanovic, 2024, p. 104). In this way, new solutions based on socio-technical systems are created, where there is mutual interpenetration and use of technology to meet the needs of society in order to neutralize climate change. In order for such solutions to be considered to be changing the conditions, there must be public acceptance in the sector proving their attractiveness. Individual-specific factors, such as environmentally friendly behavior, the relativization of climate change risks and the perception of problems, have an impact on the acceptance of such solutions. In this context, subjective norms, which are very important for all climate strategies, also have an influence (Klaus et al., 2020, p. 10). Therefore, there is currently a phenomenon of intensive searching for solutions in functional areas, including sustainable strategies oriented towards positive climate change reversing negative trends. The need for an interdisciplinary and inclusive approach to research into business strategies and climate change is gaining increasing recognition (Paul et al., 2017, p. 50). Solutions based on revolutionary changes are also triggered by the identification of the risks which companies are exposed to, taking into account factors related to climate change (Demertzidis et al., 2015, pp. 95–105). These key drivers of climate change include greenhouse gases, the sun, volcanoes and internal variability. In this context, in some situations, it is possible to use techniques based on climate change narratives, which often allow even scary scenarios to be developed. However, in business discourses, the narrative of climate change often appears more as an opportunity rather than a threat (Benites-Lazaroa et al., 2017, p. 77). Therefore, initiatives are being stimulated and recommended to find revolutionary technologies that mitigate the risk of climate change losses not only for business, but for entire societies. At the same time, a discourse based on building awareness of the multifaceted understanding of the

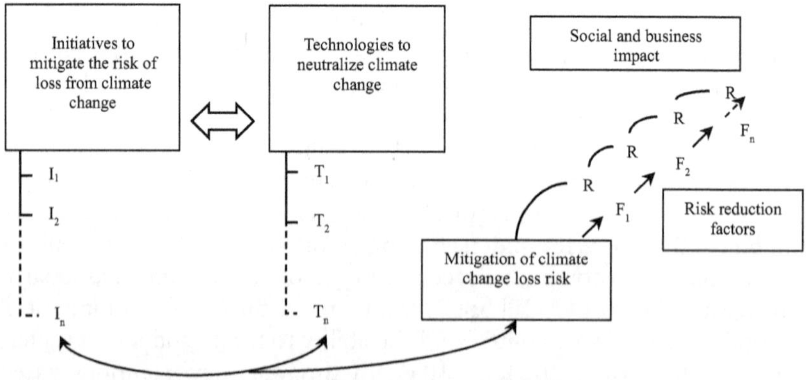

Fig. 3.1 Relationship between initiatives and technologies to reduce the risk of climate change losses (*Source* Own study)

crucial role of digital technologies and artificial intelligence in the fight against climate change prevails. Figure 3.1 shows the relationship between initiatives and technologies to reduce the risk of loss from climate change.

The experts' statements underline the urgent need for educational initiatives that offer a more holistic and sustainable perspective for the implementation of technology-based solutions, including optimizing the adverse impact of waste especially in poor countries of the world (Dwivedi et al., 2022, p. 1). The assumptions thus adopted set the course of action based on the search for breakthrough technologies that increase the chances of business market success with a positive impact on a dynamic turn towards neutralizing adverse climate change.

3.3 Digital Business Models and Cyber-Physical Systems and Their Impact on Environmental Action

The digital transformation of companies is part of the digital economy and consists of replacing traditional ways of delivering services with solutions based on digital technologies using mostly mobile devices. Action-oriented products and services supporting environmental processes and predictive systems for the capture of anomalies and weather dysfunctions and adverse changes in the natural ecosystem are core factors underlying the creation of digital business models. These models are mostly designed in the form of innovative digital platforms or solutions embedded strongly in economic sectors focused on specialized analytical, technical and forecasting services. The environmental sector is developing very dynamically in the area of attempts to find solutions to positive climate change, although it is of an embryonic nature because it meets the characteristics of an emerging area. Climate change is the subject of numerous discussions and scientific studies which clearly indicate that this process should be controlled and business activities should fit into the general trends of neutralizing this change. Digital business models, usually designed in the form of digital one-sided, bilateral or multilateral platforms, refer to a wide range of areas that can affect the following factors responsible for climate change: monitoring the greenhouse effect, monitoring the sea level rise, monitoring greenhouse gas emissions (the carbon dioxide emission curve is growing rapidly), monitoring the level of carbon dioxide concentration in the atmosphere, analyzing the difference between global warming and climate change, monitoring the rate of warming, monitoring extreme weather events, the impact of climate change on hurricanes, the impact of climate change on heat waves, the impact of climate change on droughts, the impact of climate change on fires, the impact of climate change on downpours, tornadoes and other weather anomalies. Digital platforms can also, through their built-in logical functions, support procedures for improving and optimizing energy systems. They also fit into the strategy of creating high energy efficiency, promoting the use of solar and wind energy—generally renewable energy sources. They contribute to the creation of business models based on carbon capture technologies, the development of bioenergy solutions, the creation of zero-emission energy sources, the monitoring and reduction of carbon emissions in the transport sector, the development of technologies based on alternative fuels and vehicles powered by them, the development of hydrogen technologies, the transition away from fossil fuels and a modern and innovative approach to the development of the agricultural and livestock sectors in the context of climate change minimization. Digital energy-saving applications are particularly important, as are applications for monitoring the carbon footprint, setting priorities in the investment process and diet monitoring systems for maintaining human health—generally the creation of a friendly climate. These areas are affected both directly and indirectly by the design of specific functions and performances of innovative ICT-based digital platforms, broadly based on the digital economy. For this purpose, cyber-physical systems (CPS), which are defined as computational processes that interact with a physical process, are increasingly used. They have two core layers, physical (physical, biological, etc.) and digital. In the digital layer, calculations are made on the basis of measurements/observations of physical processes. In this context, any phenomena related to climate change identified above can be observed and monitored. The results of these calculations affect the processes of the physical layer. Examples of CPS domains include advertising, entertainment/sports, aviation, environmental monitoring, agriculture, financial services, buildings, healthcare, cities, infrastructure (communication, energy and water), communities, entertainment, consumers, production, defense, science, disaster resilience, social networks, education, supply/retail chain, crisis response, transport, energy and weather (Framework for Cyber-Physical Systems,2017). All these areas are part of the strategy for deploying digital solutions to respond to climate change. Therefore, the following steps in the implementation of these solutions are required in this respect:

1. Conceptualization—What things should look like and what things should do: a set of actions that make up the CPS model (includes functional distribution, requirements and logical models).
2. Implementation—What things should be created and work: a set of activities that create, implement and support CPS (includes engineering compromises and detailed projects on a critical path to create a CPS instance) (Framework for Cyber-Physical Systems,2017).
3. Assurance—How to achieve the desired level of confidence that things will work as they should: a set of actions that ensure that the CPS operates according to the specifications (includes claims, evidence and reasoning).

Such an interpretation of the system of designing cyber-physical systems underlying the creation of digital business models conducive to climate change monitoring are innovative, serve to create climate change monitoring services and promote conscious decision-making by users that fit into the ideas contained in the functionalities of digital platforms. The combined implementation of ideas supporting projects aimed at neutralizing activities adversely affecting climate change and digital platforms for monitoring this change fill the substantive scope and underlie the development of unconventional business, analytical and research solutions.

3.4 Digital Climate Services and Their Impact on Creating New Business Spaces

Digital climate services are developing very dynamically due to the needs arising from public concern about weather changes, anomalies and dysfunctions of natural systems. Negative weather and climate trends force the search for solutions mainly based on predictive solutions for capturing potential events before they occur. In this context, a large market and demand are created for this type of solution. Such services include predictive solutions such as:

1. Systems supporting decision-making processes in the area of climate change.
2. Common climate change adaptation systems and programs that create climate knowledge.
3. Workshops and training raising public and business awareness about climate change and promoting tools and solutions used in processes supporting climate change.
4. Organizing dedicated events, festivals and study meetings promoting climate services in the traditional and online formula, raising awareness and climate sensitivity and aimed at creating interdisciplinary networks of contacts and relations in the area of climate change.
5. Integrated regional research and development programs in the area of climate change.
6. Supporting local adaptation to climate change through participatory Geoweb systems.
7. Seasonal climate and agricultural forecasts dedicated to specific locations.
8. Climate risk modeling services focused on identifying and measuring climate-related hazards and opportunities.
9. Interdisciplinary specialist climate services in the field of climate data management engineering.
10. Expert services including data analysis and model generation to develop contextual weather forecasts and related advice.

11. Offering dedicated climate and agronomic models.
12. Maps and applications providing information about the state of the climate in real time.
13. Climate change databases.
14. Services that generate climate data and forecasts.
15. Integrated advice on decision-making relating to climate change prediction and mitigation.
16. Tools that create climate projection graphs.

The services presented above set the key direction of this area of business, which in many situations is related to the work of institutions for the climate, which are supported by both the state and private sectors. Joint ventures in this area are not uncommon. There is a need to create such solutions with the participation of local government, regional and governmental units. Business creativity, on the other hand, can provide ready-made solutions which in many cases have already been validated for direct application in practice. Examples of business areas where a dynamic search for solutions for creating services affecting climate change is developing include the following:

1. The economic sector.
2. Climate and catastrophic insurance.
3. Financial services.
4. Transport and logistics services.
5. Banking and insurance services.
6. Expert services.
7. Agricultural services.
8. Climate technology design services.
9. Construction services.
10. Hydrogen production and support services.
11. Others.

Monitoring systems based on prediction, analytics and the use of Big Data seem to be a prerequisite for finding mechanisms for the effective management of the climate change process to reduce the adverse impact on the quality of life of citizens and the destruction of the earth's ecosystem. Such activities define a very wide range of new business space for the creators of startups, new business models, public–private undertakings, social initiatives, support for societies, legislation and discussions aimed at creation and technological progress and revolutions in this area.

3.5 Processes of Digital Transformation of Companies and Their Impact on the Optimization of Monitoring Environmental Change Processes

Digital transformation and the use of different types of technologies that affect all aspects of human life increase the likelihood of improving the quality of the natural environment. Digitalization may pose environmental risks, but the link between digital transformation and environmental sustainability is complex, and whether digital transformation helps or hinders environmental sustainability is a constant subject of debate in the scientific community (Truong, 2022, p. 1). Digital transformation processes consist of mapping real processes carried out in the form of a traditional virtual environment. Moving processes to the conditions of the digital economy significantly reduces pollution and the adverse impact of real processes. Global climate governance has entered a new era, and the implementation of innovative solutions in this area has become a central task (Jiang & Li, 2020, pp. 165–171); companies that adopt innovative approaches to effectively control pollution and renewable and non-renewable resource consumption and reduce their environmental impact are more involved in the fight against climate change. The higher the fossil fuel-driven growth rates, the faster the depletion of natural resources takes place. Climate governance is positively linked to the commitment to fight climate change. The deployment of eco-innovative technologies supports the integration of climate change issues in management, which can contribute to the involvement of companies in the fight against climate change (Albitar et al., 2023, p. 1). The spread of low-carbon technologies is too slow in most sectors and countries to stabilize the climate. Factors determining climate change for good are based on the following: combining behavioral change with attitudes towards creating technological innovations, seeking the potential in the assumptions of socio-technical systems as drivers of accelerated transition to a low-carbon economy and taking into account the role of digital technologies as new places for solutions to management challenges in terms of solving the problem of climate change (Matos et al., 2022, p. 1). If it is possible to carry out processes without the use of means of transport, making tangible products requiring the use of materials and raw materials (e.g., book production), carrying out many additional activities due to the lack of predictive monitoring systems, conducting real processes without the use of digital twins or simulation, the adverse impact on the environment can be significantly reduced and an ecological impact can be achieved. Industry 4.0 and Industry 5.0 solutions, lean management, the Internet of Things, artificial intelligence and many other technical solutions that are part of the technological revolution are important for processes conducive to neutralizing the impact on climate change. Projects focused on the development of technological innovations, including digital economy solutions for monitoring areas exposed to climate change risks, can monitor society's response to understand the relative effectiveness of adaptation responses to climate change. This could concern, for example, access to water and other natural resources related to climate change processes (Nyiwul, 2023, p. 1). Innovative solutions, including digital transformation mechanisms that also serve to optimize the carbon footprint, can support decision-making by companies, i.e., allow organizations to choose between alternative solutions both through value chain accounting and monitoring of external markets. The results may inspire others to change their business from focusing solely on environmental management to a driving force for sustainable development (Burek et al., 2022, p. 213). Therefore, the digital transformation significantly promotes the creation of eco-innovations, which are focused not only on reducing the adverse impact on the natural environment, but also on creating such systemic solutions that promote the creation of a new formula for understanding the implementation of innovative projects that are focused on pro-ecological activities affecting the entire business ecosystem.

3.6 Taxonomy of Digital Platforms Focused on a Positive Impact on Climate Change Towards Its Stabilization

Taxonomy refers to the system of naming and organizing things into groups with similar characteristics. Ecology, from the perspective of the definition and origin of this concept, is a branch of biology focused on the study of the relationship between species and individual organisms and their physical environment of functioning. The issue of ecology is based on a set of activities that focus on a central set of business practices including project ecology, financial ecology and ecological impact. Platform ecology does not primarily concern individual users—their ecological sensitivity—but also types of users, such as designers, managers, politicians or tourists, i.e., groups of people who share certain interests or needs in terms of ecological sensitivity. Based on the core premise of focusing on an environmentally conscious user, the concepts of opportunities and limitations on the one hand and ecological niches on the other hand further explain the functionality and strength of the social impact of platform ecology (Ibert et al., 2022). Designing a collaborative platform management model contributes to a sustainable digital platform ecosystem. In particular, encouraging green general partners and green users to join the digital platform ecosystem is a key strategy. The incentive mechanism may cover only one side of the market (general partners who co-own the company and platform users) or both sides (Calabrese et al., 2021). The taxonomy of digital platforms called green platforms classifies digital platforms by different functions and performances. The core function of these platforms is to support environmental action and positive climate change. The taxonomic approach aims to identify different types of approaches to defining digital platforms from the perspective of different criteria. These criteria can refer to both the core functions of digital platforms that indirectly affect environmental aspects and dedicated green platforms, the primary objective of which is to neutralize the adverse environmental impact, support positive climate change, build users' environmental awareness, learn based on experience and build good practices in the area of optimizing actions for minimal or even zero impact on the environment. In recent years, investment in projects to create digital platforms in the field of ecology and nature management has increased significantly. The number of solutions dedicated to products based on pro-ecological technologies used on this type of digital platforms is growing. Table 3.1 presents the proposal of a taxonomy for green digital platforms based on platform-based business model archetypes.

The proposed taxonomy based on the archetypes of various digital platforms focused on a positive impact on environmental protection, including climate change, proves that there are numerous solutions in this area which are based on different thematic areas and research space. Some are based only on pro-environmental technologies, while others

Table 3.1 Presentation of the taxonomy of ecologically oriented digital business models based on their different archetypes

No	*Green digital platform archetype*	*Description*
1	**Archetype 1: sustainable software solution**	The sustainable software solution archetype describes sustainable digital BMs that offer software to solve environmental sustainability problems for their customers. The basis of sustainable BMs is a software solution that solves specific environmental problems in BMs, business processes or private consumption with a high environmental impact. The software solution optimizes the use of customers' BM resources by reducing resource consumption, carbon emissions and waste production or enabling resource sharing
2	**Archetype 2: sustainable product–service system**	The product has a digital complement, such as IoT or mobile applications, creating a product and service system (PSS), optimizing the use of an eco-efficient product. A distinctive feature of this archetype is the use of renewable energy and reusable resources (closed loop). The digital supplement specializes in increasing the efficiency of this product (e.g., lower energy consumption) and its more efficient use (e.g., reliable harvesting). With the goal of eco-equivalence as an increasingly important criterion for purchase by customers, the companies of this archetype attempt to create a sustainable product that is fundamentally different from the competition and probably represents a new industry standard

(continued)

Table 3.1 (continued)

No	*Green digital platform archetype*	*Description*
3	**Archetype 3: sustainability intelligence**	The sustainability intelligence archetype includes purely digital, data-driven BMs that leverage the vast amounts of data currently available in combination with ecological sustainability and climate change science to provide insight into sustainability assessment and enable sustainable decision-making. The information provided by the platform enables investors to make green investment decisions. Other examples under this archetype promote real-time data monitoring, for example from an IoT sensor network, to automate the sustainable operation of the IoT network infrastructure. Technologies provide the data transparency needed to operate renewable energy networks and manage energy generation, storage and grid effectively
	Archetype 4: digital sustainable platform	Digital sustainable platforms are fully digital BMs that use multilateral markets and apply them in the context of sustainability to co-create green sustainable value with their partners. The goal of these digital sustainable platforms includes a number of SDGs, such as sufficiency by reducing food waste and responsible consumption in general, closed loops and circularity by enabling reuse and repurposing and inclusive value creation through value networking. Many of them are part of the circular economy ecosystem that seeks to give products and resources a new designation instead of wasting them. Digital sustainability platforms also encourage sustainable consumption, rewarding users for their engagement on the platform (e.g., by selling or buying second-hand items). Thanks to the points collected for transactions on the platform, users can buy discount codes or vouchers for (of course sustainable) partner companies

Source Own study based on Balabanova et al. (2021)

are directly based on conscious decisions by users to use solutions, products and services that have minimal adverse impact on the environment and derive from a conscious approach of users based on their high environmental awareness focused on a modern approach to understanding ecological issues.

3.7 Conclusions

The dynamics of the digital revolution increased particularly during and after the COVID-19 pandemic. This has revealed and unleashed incredible growth and development potential in all areas of the world. It has increased the quality of life of societies and reduced unnecessary mobility. The transformation of the economy from an analog to a digital economy has increased exponentially, which in turn has generated both positive and negative phenomena. The digital transformation and revolution have a decisively positive impact on reducing and neutralizing the adverse impact on the climate. The combined implementation of the principles of digital and climate transformation creates a platform and a new trajectory for controlling socio-technical systems in many directions. This determines a new shape of understanding the economy and its place in the system of social relations.

References

Albitar, K., Al-Shaer, H., & Liu, Y. S. (2023). Corporate commitment to climate change: The effect of eco-innovation and climate governance. *Research Policy, 52*, 1.

Balabanova, A., Keschyaan, N., Borisova, T., & Hachemizova, E. (2021). Using digital platforms for environmental management. *E3S Web of Conferences, 244*, 07006. https://doi.org/10.1051/e3sconf/202124407006, EMMFT-2020.

Benites-Lazaroa, L. L., Mello-Théryb, N. A., & Lahsena, M. (2017). Business storytelling about energy and climate change: The case of Brazil's ethanol industry. *Energy Research & Social Science, 31*, 77.

Burek, J., Bauer, C., Kirchain, R., Moore, E., Gregory, J., & Norris, G. (2022). Assessing handprint potentials for business's eco-innovation. *Sustainable Production and Consumption, 29*, 213.

Calabrese, M., La Sala, A., Patrick Fuller, R., & Laudando, A. (2021). Digital platform ecosystems for sustainable innovation: Toward a new meta-organizational model. *Administrative Science, Nr., 11*, 119. https://doi.org/10.3390/admsci11040119

Demertzidis, N., Tsalis, T. A., Loupa, G., & Nikolaou, I. E. (2015). A benchmarking framework to evaluate business climate change risks: A practical tool suitable for investors decision-making process. *Climate Risk Management, 10*, 95–105.

Dwivedi, Y. K., Hughes, L., Kumar Kar, A., Baabdullah, A. M., Grover, P., Abbas, R., Andreini, D., Abumoghli, I., Barlette, Y., Bunkerl, D., Chandra Krus, L., Constantiou, I., Davison, R.M., De, R., Dubey, R., Fenby-Taylor, H., Gupta, B., He, W., Kodama, M., Mantymaki, M., Metri, B., Michael, K., Olaisen, J., Panteli, N., Pekkola, S., Nishant, R., Raman, R., Rana, N. P., Rowe, F., Sarker, S., Scholtz, B., Sein, M., Dharmeshkumar Shah, J., Teo, T. S. H., Kumar Tiwari, M., Thanning Vendelø, M., & Wade, M. (2022). Climate change and COP26: Are digital technologies and information management part of the problem or the solution? An editorial reflection and call to action. *International Journal of Information Management, 63, 1.*

Framework for Cyber-Physical Systems: Volume 1, Overview Version 1.0, NIST Special Publication 1500–201, Cyber-Physical Systems Public Working Group Smart Grid and Cyber-Physical Systems Program Office Engineering Laboratory. (2025). National Institute of Standards and Technology Special Publication 1500–201 Natl. Inst. Stand. Technol. Spec. Publ. 1500–201, 79 pages, CODEN: NSPUE2. Retrieved 18 January, 2025, from, https://doi.org/10.6028/NIST.SP.1500-201

Ibert, O., Oechslen, A., Repenning, A., & Schmidt, S. (2022). Platform ecology: A user-centric and relational conceptualization of online platforms. *Global Networks, 22*, 564–579.

Jiang, S., & Li, J. (2020). Global climate governance in the new era: Potential of business actors and technological innovation, *Chinese Journal of Population. Resources and Environment, 18*, 165–171.

Klaus, G., Ernst, A., & Oswald, L. (2020). Psychological factors influencing laypersons' acceptance of climate. *Technology in Society, 60*, Article 101222.

Matos, S., Viardot, E., Sovacool, B. K., Geels, F. W., & Xiong, Y. (2022). Innovation and climate change: A review and introduction to the special issue. *Technovation, 117*, 1.

Nyiwul, L. (2023). Climate change adaptation innovation in the water sector in Africa: Dataset. *Data in Brief, 46*, 1.

Paul, A., Lang, J. W. B., & Baumgartner, R. J. (2017). A multilevel approach for assessing business strategies on climate change. *Journal of Cleaner Production, 160*, 50.

Ritala, P., & Jovanovic, M. (2024). Platformizers, orchestrators, and guardians: Three types of B2B platform business models. In A. Aagaard (Ed.), *Business Model Innovation Game Changers and Contemporary Issues* (p. 104). Palgrave Macmillan imprint is published by the registered company Springer Nature Switzerland AG.

Truong, T. C. (2022). The impact of digital transformation on environmental sustainability. *Hindawi Advances in Multimedia*, (1)Article ID 6324325, 12 pages. https://doi.org/10.1155/2022/6324325

CHAPTER 4

The Place and Role of the Energy and Climate Revolution in the Relevant Literature

Abstract The aim of this chapter is to present place and role of the energy and climate revolution in the relevant literature. The adopted mechanisms of energy policy-making significantly impact climate change in both negative and positive terms. Optimal power systems are sought by scientists and practitioners on a continuous basis. This is not an easy task because it depends on numerous variables determining the final results of these processes. The energy revolution can be seen as a time of technological development, with breakthrough development in the generation, transmission and use of energy, leading to a radical change in industry, transport and everyday life. This is happening in the world today through dynamic transformation processes. The energy transition visibly transforms the structure of energy mixes and gives them a different level of importance and impact on the economy, business and society than before. This type of action is determined by expectations of a change of thinking in the field of reducing various types of emissions to the climate in global and local terms. Therefore, such activities should be based on the principles of scientific cognition. In this space, reliable and effective solutions can be developed to link fossil-fuel power generation with the principles and solutions of distributed energy.

Keywords Energy · Climate revolution · Impact climate change · Energy revolution · Technological development

A. Jabłoński and M. Jabłoński, *Digital Business Models and Environmental Action*,
https://doi.org/10.1007/978-3-032-15298-5_4

4.1 Introduction

The adopted mechanisms of energy policy-making significantly impact climate change in both negative and positive terms. Optimal power systems are sought by scientists and practitioners on a continuous basis. This is not an easy task because it depends on numerous variables determining the final results of these processes. The energy revolution can be seen as a time of technological development, with breakthrough development in the generation, transmission and use of energy, leading to a radical change in industry, transport and everyday life. This is happening in the world today through dynamic transformation processes. The energy transition visibly transforms the structure of energy mixes and gives them a different level of importance and impact on the economy, business and society than before. This type of action is determined by expectations of a change of thinking in the field of reducing various types of emissions to the climate in global and local terms. Therefore, such activities should be based on the principles of scientific cognition. In this space, reliable and effective solutions can be developed to link fossil fuel power generation with the principles and solutions of distributed energy.

4.2 Electrical Power Engineering in Shaping Climate Responsibility

Electrical power engineering plays one of the most crucial roles in shaping the climate responsibility of the economy, business and society. Electrical power engineering is understood as the field of electrical engineering dealing with the generation, transmission, distribution and use of electrical energy. The energy transformation is entering a decisive phase of technological and organizational changes by changing the structures of optimal power mixes. In this space, it is crucial to identify the right relationship between fossil fuel energy and energy produced from renewable energy sources. Currently, in scientific and practical terms, various types of energy solutions are sought, which are the best possible solutions in economic–financial, technological and organizational–management terms, mainly in structures of hybrid application of various types of energy. Thus, a significant energy revolution is created which is connected with the implemented principles of climate transformation. Energy is now becoming the key word for building positive energy and climate communities that understand the shrinking of natural resources and the emergence of new opportunities and energy opportunities caused, among others, by dynamic climate change. The threat of heat waves, frost, snow, wind, drought and hail are the factors that determine a whole range of strategic and tactical–operational actions influencing the scope of decisions made in this area.

4.3 Different Structures of Energy Mixes as a Platform for the Energy Revolution in Climate Adaptation Change

Conducting the correct decision-making processes in the area of energy transformation is not simple and unambiguous. This is an extremely complex process because it is based on the logic of both global and local approaches. From a global perspective, it includes the applicable formal and legal requirements and trends in economic and social development, while from a local perspective, it includes the resource opportunities resulting from the potential that can be applied to the production of various types of energy. This approach leads to the construction of the so-called energy mix with a different structure, which can be homogeneous or hybrid. An energy mix can be interpreted as the generation of appropriate proportions and types of energy sources used to generate electrical energy in a given country, region or power system. The core attribute of this decision-making system is the criterion of energy security, the stability of this system and the resource potential. The energy mix is important and crucial to achieving an acceptable level of energy security, reasonable energy production costs and the direct and indirect impact on the environment and CO_2 emissions. Often, in the field of energy security, an energy mix is sought that will ensure its energy self-sufficiency in a given region. The stability criterion seeks systems that ensure an adequate level of continuity of energy supply, which is relatively simple as regards fossil fuel and requires the construction of energy storage facilities for the use of renewable energy. The resource potential, on the other hand, results from the location of resources (fossil fuels) and weather possibilities (a large number of sunny days, blowing winds, etc.). All this makes it possible to create different energy mixes with different percentages of different types of energy. Table 4.1 presents selected structures of energy mixes with recommendations and the most suitable business models for them.

Table 4.1 Selected structures of energy mixes with recommendations and the most suitable business models for them

Type of energy mix	*Share of different energy sources*	*Examples of countries*	*Climate and adaptation recommendations*	*The most suitable business model of companies*	*Bibliographic sources*
1. Carbon (traditional)	60–80% coal, 10–20% gas, 5–10% RES, 0–10% other	Poland (until 2015), South Africa	Urgent decarbonization; investments in RES and nuclear; support for coal regions	**Transformational model:** coal phase-out, portfolio diversification (RES + atom), employment restructuring	J. Jurasz, F.A. Canales, A. Kies, M. Guezgouz, A. Beluco, A review on the complementarity of renewable energy sources: Concept, metrics, application and future research directions, Solar Energy, Volume 195, 1 January 2020, Pages 703–724, https://https://doi.org/10.1016/j.solener.2019.11.087, Erdiwansyah et al. Protection and Control of Modern Power Systems (2021) 6:3 https://doi.org/10.1186/s41601-021–00,181-3, Hans-Kristian Ringkjøb, Peter M. Haugan, Ida Marie Solbrekke, A review of modelling tools for energy and electricity systems with large shares of variable renewables, Renewable and Sustainable Energy Reviews 96 (2018) 440–459, https://doi.org/10.1016/j.rser.2018.08.002, Sarah Becker, Bethany A. Frew, Gorm B. Andresen, Timo Zeyer, Stefan Schramm, Martin Greiner, Mark Z. Jacobson, Features of a fully renewable US electricity system: Optimized mixes of wind and solar PV and transmission grid extensions, Energy, Volume 72, 1 August 2014, Pages 443–458, https://doi.org/10.1016/j.energy.2014.05.067, Stefan Weitemeyer, David Kleinhans, Thomas Vogt, Carsten Agert, Integration of Renewable Energy Sources in future power systems: The role of storage, Renewable Energy Volume 75, March 2015, Pages 14–20, https://doi.org/10.1016/j.renene.2014.09.028, Edoardo Barabino, Davide Fioriti, Emanuele Guerrazzi, Ivan Mariuzzo, Davide Poli, Marco Raugi, Ehsan Razaei, Eva Schito, Dimitri Thomopulos, Energy Communities: A review on trends, energy system modelling, business models, and optimization objectives, Sustainable Energy, Grids and Networks 36 (2023) 101,187, https://doi.org/10.1016/j.segan.2023.101187, Małek, A.; Marciniak, A.; Bednarczyk, T. Probabilistic Analysis of Electricity Production from a Photovoltaic–Wind Energy Mix for Sustainable Transport Needs. Sustainability 2024, 16, 10,164. https://doi.org/10.3390/su16231 0164, Gitelman, L.; Kozhevnikov, M. New Business Models in the Energy Sector in the Context of Revolutionary Transformations. Sustainability 2023, 15, 3604. https://doi.org/10.3390/su15043604

Type of energy mix	*Share of different energy sources*	*Examples of countries*	*Climate and adaptation recommendations*	*The most suitable business model of companies*	*Bibliographic sources*
2. Gas–carbon (transformation)	30–50% gas, 20–40% carbon, 20–30% RES, 0–10% atomic/hydro	Italy, Turkey	Reduction of coal; development of RES and biogas; CCS; diversification of fuels	**Hybrid model:** utility + RES + warehouses; development of flexibility services	
3. Nuclear–carbon	40–70% atomic, 20–40% carbon, 5–15% RES, 0–10% gas	Czech Republic, Slovakia, Bulgaria	Reduction of coal, development of SMR and RES; recycling of radioactive waste	**Infrastructure model:** State investment in nuclear and networks	
4. Nuclear–RES (low-carbon)	30–50% atomic, 30–50% RES, 10–20% gas, 0–5% coal/oil	France	Development of offshore wind and PV; hydrogen; maintaining the atom	**Dual model:** large operators (atom) + investors in RES	
5. RES–gas (transitional)	40–60% RES, 30–40% gas, 5–10% coal/oil, 0–10% atomic	Spain, United Kingdom	Energy storage and hydrogen; elimination of gas; civic energy	**Prosumer and innovative model:** micro-installations, energy clusters	
6. Dominant RES (decarbonization)	70–90% RES, 10–20% gas/hydrogen, 0–10% atomic	Denmark, Portugal, Norway	Smart grid, hydrogen, offshore wind	**Network and technology model:** offshore companies + IT/IoT integrators	

(continued)

Table 4.1 (continued)

Type of energy mix	*Share of different energy sources*	*Examples of countries*	*Climate and adaptation recommendations*	*The most suitable business model of companies*	*Bibliographic sources*
7. Zero-emission target (2050 +)	40–60% RES, 30–50% atomic, 0–20% hydrogen/warehouse/imported, 0% fossil fuels	Vision for the EU 2050	Net zero; circular economy; hydrogen	**Integrated model:** multi-utility, PPP, circular economy	
8. Regional	Hydro: 80–95% hydro Geothermal: 50–80% geothermal Oil/gas: 80–90% oil/gas	Norway, Costa Rica (hydro) Iceland (geothermal) Saudi Arabia, Qatar (oil/gas)	Hydro/geothermal → export know-how; oil/gas → diversification and RES	**Export or diversification model:** export of hydro/geothermal technologies, transformation of raw material economies	

Source Own study

The structures of energy mixes with recommendations and the most suitable business models presented in the table above primarily show how many possibilities of modeling the energy potential are suitable for the needs, possibilities and benefits. Therefore, it seems appropriate to use a scientific approach to search for the best possible solutions in this important transformational area as well as a multidimensional economic approach in the field of optimization and to search for all methods of efficient management of energy resources.

4.4 Clean Energy as a Tool for Creating Positive Climate Change Towards a Clean Climate by Climate-Responsible Companies

Energy and efficient and effective energy management are mandatory and inseparable attributes of the adequate quality of human life around the world. Without energy and a systematic energy supply today, it is in fact impossible to function in any way in the modern world. Energy always increases prosperity and improves the comfort of people in their existence. The richer the country, the more energy it consumes. Wealth is measured, among others, by the potential for energy consumption, but this generates an increased amount of carbon dioxide. The use of clean energy leads to the achievement of a clean climate. The clean climate concept should be supported by solutions for cleaner production which have been in use for many years. The principles of cleaner production are used as waste minimization, pollution prevention and eco-efficiency, based on four Rs: Reduction, Recycling, Reuse and Repurpose. Technological solutions in the field of energy strongly determine the possibilities and opportunities of positive climate change. This is particularly related to the energy transition pertaining, among others, to the creation and use of new and renewable energy sources, often called clean energy. This pertains to achieving high energy efficiency in terms of countries, cities, regions, businesses and households. An appropriate energy mix, including a specific and justified structure of renewable and non-renewable energy resources, must be defined in an economically, socially, technologically and climate-relevant manner. Activities aimed at developing nuclear energy and, among others, investing in natural gas, solar energy or wind energy can serve this purpose. Gas is considered to be less harmful than other sources of energy. Social governance (SG) is important here, playing an important role in and bearing responsibility for promoting a democratic, fair, healthy and sustainable economy and society, where most of the energy is used for heating and lighting residential and commercial buildings and transport and industry in energy-oriented cities. In an energy-oriented city, residents enjoy a high quality of life thanks to the efficient use of resources and a low-carbon footprint. Due to the high complexity of energy-oriented systems and their critical importance, energy management is one of the most difficult problems in these metropolitan centers and carries a promise of a political response. Sustainability is the promise of social governance that coordinates this response. Sustainability can only be achieved through effective governance (Ji & Huang, 2022). Clean energy is often achieved through renewable energy sources (RES), which today are primarily a key alternative to exploited fossil fuels and at the same time are perceived as an important factor determining and conducive to stopping dangerous anomalies, dysfunctions and climate extremes on earth. One should be aware that the production of energy from RES takes place in a decentralized manner and is a form of distributed energy aimed mainly at the self-sufficiency of the region. RES involve the citizen—the prosumer—in the co-creation and exchange of energy. This is a specific and strong empowerment of the customer–prosumer as the recipient and co-producer of energy. However, it should be remembered that the energy transition is not only about moving away from carbon-intensive fuels, but is today primarily about developing a number of opportunities for the development of renewable energy sources. Regulatory and legal stability is fundamental to all ongoing investments in renewable energy sources. The degree and extent of complexity of the required regulatory and administrative procedures, and the scope and stability of supporting and strengthening the development of renewable energy, strongly affect the attractiveness of these very important energy and climate investments. When in line with the development of the company, it is required to build individualized climate capital within the organization in a systemic way. A strong strengthening catalyst thereof can be climate culture jointly shaped in the organization. This culture should be based on artifacts resulting from storytelling.

4.5 Climate Engineering in Shaping Climate Responsibility

The engineering and technical approach to climate change is one of the foundations of climate truth. This climate truth derives from science. Management based on physics and mathematics offers significant substantive value, not only for climatologists. Climate change knowledge and awareness foster intellectual development processes. The climate crisis and resulting consequences for the natural ecosystem create a new context for the development of science and practice. This manifests itself through dynamic changes that are noticeable on a daily basis. This is related to emerging new environmental regulations, violent atmospheric phenomena, but also political, social and economic changes that require rapid adaptation to new existential conditions. Climatology, the scientific study of the climate that involves the analysis and understanding of patterns and changes in weather conditions and atmospheric phenomena over long periods, is important here. It covers a wide range of scientific disciplines, including meteorology, hydrology, oceanography, geography and geology, and uses a variety of tools and techniques such as statistical analysis, computer modeling and remote sensing. Climatology aims to provide insight into how the climate system functions, how it changed in the past and how it can evolve in the future. The science supporting the principles of climatology is climate engineering, which can be understood as a set of technologies, solutions, methods and techniques aimed at the effective and efficient management of the climate systems of the Earth as a planet to counteract dynamically occurring climate change. Climate geoengineering can be defined as a large-scale modification of the Earth's weather and environment to combat global warming. In this case, it is assumed that climate change is the result of industrial human activity, which emits very large amounts of carbon dioxide into the atmosphere causing the warming of the Earth. Climate engineering solutions should be based on an interdisciplinary decision-making and substantive platform. The idea is to combine problem-solving approaches to generate the best possible climate outcome using suitable, dedicated innovative climate technologies.

In terms of application, climate technologies can be divided into three groups (regardless of sector):

- directly reducing or eliminating emissions to water, soil and air,
- helping to adapt to the effects of climate change in the long and short term,
- helping to understand the impact of climate change based on the data collected and the processed and generated results.

Technology governance should be implemented in a systemic manner that sets out core milestones to ensure that it achieves its intended results in this area.

The basic scope of the technological roadmap covers three areas, namely:

1. Identifying potential markets where newly developed products used currently or in the future may apply.
2. Identifying the types of products resulting from the technologies used.
3. The choice of technologies used (Fig. 4.1).

The final product of using technological roadmaps is the integration of partial technological roadmaps into one integrated map constituting the resulting model of the company's technological strategy. If a technological revolution is applied to solutions used in the fight against climate change, it should result in the development of a new product or group of products and services conducive to positive climate change and finding a potentially new market for them. Finding an outlet for these new services will not be easy, as it requires increasing awareness of the entire business environment, changes in legislation and demonstrating a significant demand for such services due to broad societal expectations. The relationship between revolutionary technologies and attractive markets for new products and services must be internally coherent and socially acceptable. The final technological roadmap is a graphical representation of the company's technological strategy. The company's technological strategies are currently the foundation for building competitive advantages and creating new solutions in the sphere of the new digital economy. Old approaches to strategy have limited application due to the digital

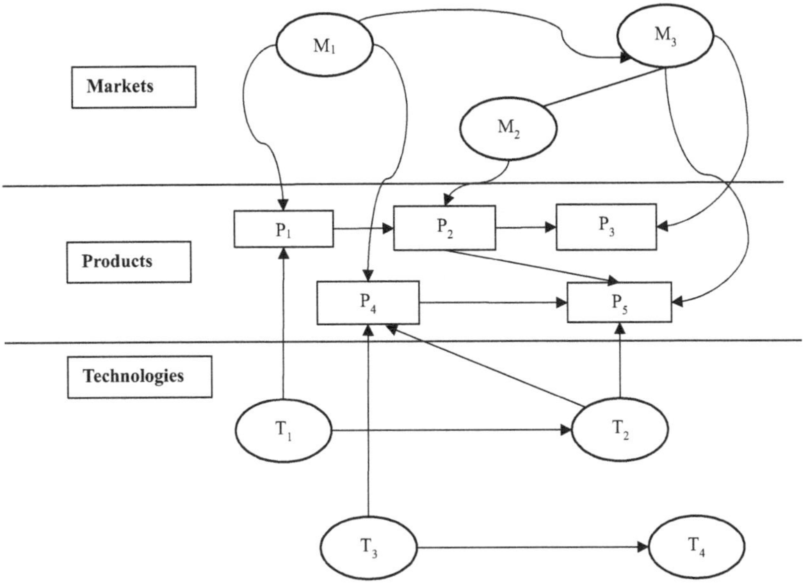

Fig. 4.1 Generic technology roadmap (*Source* Rinne [2004, p. 69])

nature of business models, where technology stimulates the possibilities of expansion of solutions and their acceptance by recipients. Incomprehensible strategies due to underdeveloped technologies will not be implemented. Technology stimulates their effectiveness and attractiveness for managers interested in new business creation spaces. M. Rinne defined four models of technological roadmaps, each of which has a different configuration of activities in the area of technologies, products and markets. In his opinion, technological roadmaps combine technologies, products and markets, thus achieving a high level of abstract thinking among managers enabling them to develop innovations and translate them into products and markets. He also believes that a company is a complex group of elements that maintain the business model in permanence against the factors of the external and internal environment, which, due to disturbances often resulting from inclusive business models, i.e., those that result from changes in the law, are constantly changing and are subjected to dynamic adaptations to the variability and complexity of the environment. In the face of changes in the external and internal environment, especially in terms of macroeconomic changes, these models are subject to destabilization and constant adaptation up to the point of full, certainly temporary, market acceptance, and at such a rhythm they require constant adjustments in the technology–product/service–market relationship. Putting emphasis on innovation and the dynamic transformation thereof into products serves to conquer new markets while strengthening the core value driver, which is sales growth. It is worth noting that among the many elements constituting business models, product innovation, which is a core area of technological roadmaps, stimulates the interaction of these solutions with the environment in order to improve the mechanisms for adapting them to the current, constantly changing needs of highly demanding customers. This can be achieved by building a climate strategic technology map and a roadmap for the development of climate technologies (Fig. 4.2).

In the presented roadmap for the development of climate technologies, three core components correlate, namely climate technologies, climate

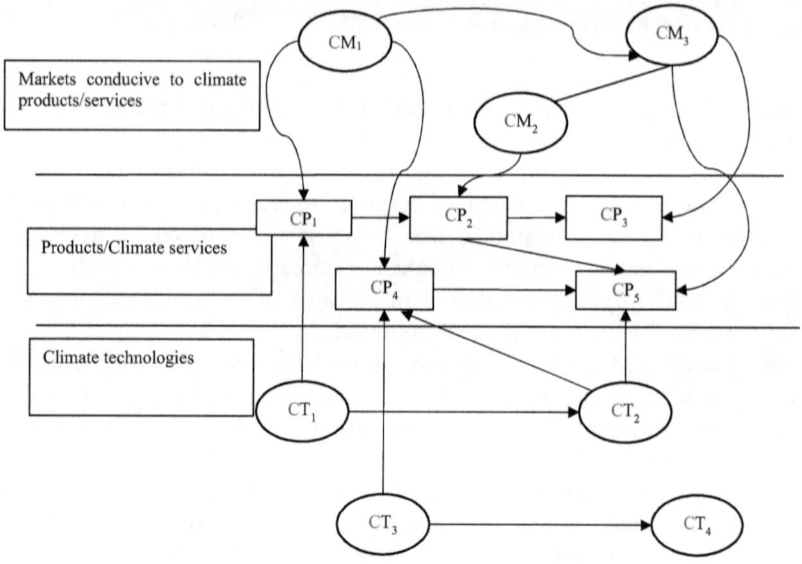

Fig. 4.2 Roadmap for the development of climate technologies (*Source* Own study based on Rinne [2004, p. 69])

products/services and markets conducive to climate products/services. This dependency cascade should materialize and intertwine with an appropriate feedback loop guaranteeing a permanent, continuous cycle of strategic renewal towards the opening of new perspectives and spaces for climate innovation. Such a dynamic system ensures that the proper dynamics of shaping and changing market behavior are maintained both at the level of the organization and stakeholders centered around it who are open to climate adaptation in terms of positive strategic goals. At the same time, it helps prove the truth and rely on scientific evidence supported by reliable scientific research published in reputable scientific journals. This is confirmed by the experience of the Climate Technology Center and Network (CTCN) (https://www.ctc-n.org/) in Tidal River Management (TRM) and the work on Technology Needs Assessments (TNA) and the National Adaptation Plan (NAP), which resulted in a wide range of assessments at the technological level in terms of the following:

(a) How they contribute to the Sustainable Development Goals of developing countries, with lower emissions and the highest resilience to climate change;
(b) What the barriers are to their implementation on a larger scale in the country context;
(c) What measures can be taken to remove these barriers;
(d) How these actions create a coherent path to the desired future of a given country and sector.

Technology Needs Assessments (TNAs) are long-term and evolving processes under the UNFCCC that are based on a comprehensive, national, participatory and action-oriented approach. They identify and prioritize the technologies needed to adapt to and mitigate climate change in different sectors of developing countries. NAPs are National Adaptation Plan (NAP) documents (CTCN https://www.ctc-n.org/).

An example of such a technology map is a technology roadmap highlighting technological opportunities for low-carbon technologies in energy-intensive industries, including the use of green energy and hydrogen and identifying available support instruments, synergies and actions to accelerate the transformation. It calls for dialogue with Member States and regions on their specific, common and cross-border interests and needs, and provides a comprehensive contribution to European decision-makers (ERA Industrial Technology Roadmap, 2022). Another example of such a technology map is the carbon capture and storage (CCS) roadmap, which for the first time identifies a detailed technology development scenario from a handful of large projects today to more than 3000 projects by 2050. It states that the next decade will be a key breakthrough period for CCS; governments, industry and public stakeholders need to act quickly to demonstrate CCS on a large scale around the world in a variety of contexts. The roadmap ends with a set of short-term actions that stakeholders will need to take to achieve the vision of the road map. The International Energy Agency (IEA) presents this roadmap not only to provide additional focus and urgency to international discussions on the importance of CCS as a technology solution, but also to set a course that will make CCS a reality worldwide (Technology Roadmap, 2010).

4.6 Fighting Climate Change by Developing Management Systems Based on Standardization

The adaptation of companies to physical climate risks can be compared to the cycle of growth, contraction, decline and reorganization observed in disrupted natural ecosystems. Therefore, the condition for designing digital business models from the perspective of the conceptualization and operationalization of modern business mechanisms conditioned by climate change is knowledge of standards, norms and legal provisions pertaining to this complex issue. The question may be posed as to whether we use business as usual in the context of the problems of the climate crisis or modern, innovative, creative and smart climate-based business instead. Standards that can be used to identify climate problems and solutions, as well as approaches to creating mechanisms to neutralize adverse impact on climate change, cover a wide range of issues, several of which are discussed in this part of the chapter. One of the most popular standards used in business is ISO 9001:2015 (ISO9001:2015, 2021). The planned amendment of this standard addresses the problem of climate change, which is becoming increasingly visible and felt around the world, affecting various aspects of the organization's activities. Their inclusion in the requirements of the standards for the certification of management systems is stated in the information declarations published in 2024. The International Organization for Standardization (ISO) adopted a resolution that added two new statements to a number of current standards for management systems, which will also be taken into account in all new standards under development/verification. Changes (two new statements) indicate the need to consider the impact of climate change on the ability to achieve the intended results of the management system. Core theses included in these projects include, but are not limited to, the issues of understanding the organization and its context. The organization should identify external and internal issues that are relevant to its purpose and that affect the ability of its management system to achieve the intended results. The organization should determine whether climate change is an important issue. It should be taken into account in the climate change management system and the assumption that it is an external factor so important to the expert community of quality management of products and services that it should not be omitted from the analysis. It is important to determine how climate change can affect an organization's ability to achieve its intended results, rather than what companies can do to mitigate the impact of climate change (although this may be a side effect or an indirect result of taking risks/opportunities into account). Organizations can address climate change issues by complementing their current context analysis, during management reviews, adding climate change risks to their risk analysis, launching related projects and undertaking specific actions, etc.

1. **Supply chain disruptions:** Climate change can lead to extreme weather events such as floods, droughts and storms that can disrupt supply chains. For ISO 9001-compliant QMS, this may affect the ability to consistently deliver products and services that meet customer requirements and applicable statutory and regulatory requirements.
2. **Availability of ecosystem resources and services:** Climate change can affect the availability of natural resources that are critical to production processes. A quality management system must be adaptable to these changes to ensure the efficient use of resources and maintenance of product quality.
3. **Compliance:** With a growing focus on environmental protection, there are more regulations related to climate change and sustainable development. Certified organizations must ensure that their quality management system complies with changing regulatory requirements to avoid legal issues, ensure compliance and maintain their reputation.

4. **Customer requirements and expectations:** Customers are becoming increasingly environmentally aware and expect companies to adopt sustainable practices. To ensure continuous customer satisfaction, an ISO 9001-compliant quality management system must take into account these changing customer expectations.
5. **Other:** e.g., related to labor productivity and changes in production costs, impact on opportunities and business models (https://www.pcbc.gov.pl/en/blog/certification/changes-climate-a-requirements-iso-9001 2025).

Other technical standards also address a number of other issues related to this issue. The objective of the 'Adaptation to climate change—Principles, requirements and guidelines' standard is to ensure that an organization assesses its ability to take the actions specified in the requirements of this standard by:

- defining the leadership and broader management required for the organization's climate change adaptation process;
- identifying the human resources required, including the human resources of any project teams involved;
- defining roles and responsibilities;
- identifying the need for financial resources;
- identifying the required levels of expertise and experience, as well as sources of information and data;
- identifying the moments when an organization makes strategic decisions.

The organization should:

- document the results of its assessment, including any capability gaps;
- establish a work program to address these gaps;
- commit human and financial resources to undertake this work program;
- identify relevant stakeholders;
- develop a cooperation plan with relevant stakeholders to understand their needs and expectations in relation to climate change adaptation (ISO14090:2019(E)).

Another standard that sets the directions for logical action to neutralize climate change is the International Standard ISO 14091—Adaptation to climate change—Guidelines on vulnerability, impacts and risk assessment. This document provides guidance for assessing the risks associated with the potential impacts of climate change. It describes how to understand vulnerability and how to develop and implement a robust climate change risk assessment. It can be used to assess both current and future climate change risks (ISO 14091:2021(E)). The risk assessment in this document provides the basis for planning, implementing, monitoring and evaluating climate change adaptation for each organization, regardless of its size, type and nature. This group of standards also includes a standard addressing the issue of establishing an approach and methodology for a country-based mechanism to channel climate finance to subnational authorities to support climate change adaptation and enhance local resilience, thereby contributing to the objectives of the 2015 Paris Agreement of the United Nations Framework Convention on Climate Change (UNFCCC) and the United Nations Sustainable Development Goals (SDGs). The country-based mechanism uses performance-based climate resilience grants (PBCRGs), which provide programming and verification of climate change spending at the local level, offering strong incentives to improve performance in terms of increased resilience.

This International Standard ISO 14093 (ISO14093:2022(E)) provides requirements and guidelines and applies to organizations such as national and subnational authorities, donors, companies, financial institutions and international organizations that are involved in implementing a country-based mechanism to channel climate finance to subnational authorities to support climate change adaptation and resilience. As part of the development of standardization in the area of climate change, there is another standard, namely the International Standard ISO 14097 (ISO 14097:2021(E)), which deals with the general framework, including principles, requirements and guidelines for the assessment, measurement, monitoring and reporting of investments and financial activities in relation to climate change and the transition to a low-carbon economy. The evaluation includes the following elements:

- the compatibility (or lack thereof) of the investment and financial decisions taken by the financier with low-carbon transition pathways, adaptation pathways and climate objectives;

- the impact of actions taken through the financier's investment and lending decisions on achieving climate goals in the real economy, i.e., mitigation (greenhouse gas emissions) and adaptation (resilience);
- risks for owners of financial assets (e.g., private equity, listed shares, bonds and loans) arising from climate change.

To support the financier's assessment of the impact of investment and loan decisions, this document provides guidance to the financier on how to:

- set targets and define indicators to be used to track the progress of the low-carbon transition pathways of the entities in which it invests;
- identify low-carbon transition and adaptation trajectories for investors;
- document the cause-and-effect relationship or link between climate action and its results, effects and impacts.

This document applies to funders, i.e., investors and lenders. It directs their reporting activities to the following third parties: shareholders, customers, decision-makers, financial regulators and NGOs. International Standard ISO 19115–1 (ISO19115-1:2014(E)) defines the schema required to describe geographic information and services using metadata. It provides information on identification, scope, quality, spatial and temporal aspects, content, spatial references, representation, distribution and other characteristics of digital geographic data and services. This part of ISO 19115 applies to:

- cataloguing all types of resources, clearing house activities and a full description of data sets and services;
- geographical services, geographical data sets, series of data sets and individual geographical characteristics and characteristics.

This standard defines:

- mandatory and conditional metadata sections, metadata units and metadata elements;

- the minimum set of metadata required to support most metadata applications (searching for data, determining the suitability of data for use, data access, data transfer and use of digital data and services);
- optional metadata elements allowing for a more extensive standard description of resources, if required;
- a method for expanding metadata to fit specialized needs.

Although this part of ISO 19115 applies to digital data and services, its principles can be extended to many other types of resources, such as maps, charts and text documents, as well as non-geographic data. Some conditional metadata elements may not apply to these other forms of data. In order of importance, the International Standard ISO 19115–2 (ISO19115-2:2019(E)) is relevant to climate change. The purpose of this standard is to extend ISO 19115–1:2014, defining the scheme required for an extended description of the acquisition and processing of geographic information, including images. It covers the characteristics of measurement systems and the numerical methods and calculation procedures used to derive geographical information from the data obtained by them. This document also includes XML encoding for the acquisition and processing of metadata, thereby extending the XML schemas defined in ISO/TS 19,115–3. In turn, the International Standard ISO 19131 (ISO19131:2022(E)) is applicable to the description of requirements for the specification of geographical data products, based on the concepts of other International Standards of the ISO 19100 family of standards. It also provides guidance on creating specifications for data products so that they are easy to understand and fit for purpose. This document specifies the XML encoding of the data product specifications and provides a representation of the Web Ontology Language (OWL) of the underlying United Modeling Language (UML) model. The standard is intended for use by data manufacturers, data providers, service providers and potential users of data products. For the further development of this issue, another standard on climate change is applicable, namely the International Standard ISO 19156 (ISO19156:2023(E)), the scope of which concerns the definition of the conceptual scheme for observations, the characteristics involved in the observation process and the characteristics involved in sampling during observation. They provide models for the exchange of information describing observational acts and their results, both within and between different scientific and technical communities. Observations typically involve sampling the final feature of interest. This document defines a common set of sample types according to their spatial, material (in the case of *ex situ* observations) or statistical nature. The diagram covers the relationship between the characteristics of the sample (sub-sampling, derived samples).

This standard applies only to externally visible interfaces and does not impose any restrictions on basic implementations other than those needed to meet interface specifications in a real situation. The next International Standard ISO 19157 (ISO19157:2013(E)) aims to establish principles for describing the quality of geographical data:

- it defines the components to describe the quality of the data;
- it specifies the components and structure of the contents of the register for data quality measures;
- it describes the general procedures for assessing the quality of geographical data;
- it establishes rules for data quality reporting.

This International Standard also defines a set of data quality measures to be used in assessing and reporting data quality. It applies to data producers providing quality information to describe and assess the extent to which the dataset complies with the product specification, as well as to data users trying to determine whether specific geographical data are of sufficient quality for their specific use. This International Standard does not attempt to define minimum acceptable quality levels for geographical data. Proving the number of standardization documents for attempts to address climate change, one cannot fail to mention the International Standard ISO 32210 (ISO 32210:2022(E)), the assumption of which is that it provides guidance to organizations on the use of overriding principles, practices and terminology for sustainable development in financial activities. It deals with relevant issues from the perspective of the organization and its stakeholders.

This document applies to all organizations active in the financial sector, including but not limited to direct lenders and investors, asset managers and service providers. In addition to financial institutions and intermediaries, this document may be used by other parties in the financial sector, such as suppliers or recipients of sustainable finance, government organizations, public and private sector institutions, economic entities, industry associations, financial market regulators and supervisory and control authorities. In the context of further exploration of knowledge of climate change standardization, the Technical Specification ISO/TS 19,158 (ISO/TS 19,158:2012(E)), which deals with the establishment of a quality assurance framework specific to geographical information, should not be overlooked. It is based on the quality principles and procedures for assessing the quality of geographical information set out in ISO 19157 and the general principles of quality management set out in ISO 9000.

The framework set out in this Technical Specification allows the customer to ensure that his/her suppliers, both internal and external, are able to provide geographic information of the required quality. The framework is based on ensuring the supplier's ability to understand and meet quality requirements. Through the quality assurance framework, both the customer and the supplier can consider the required quality at the earliest opportunity in the production/update process. The rules and obligations of the customer–supplier relationship are presented, which facilitates the framework. Responsibility for the quality assessment procedure is shared between the customer and the supplier. This Technical Specification applies to customers and suppliers of all geographic information where product quality may be compromised by supplier processes in any of the following scenarios:

- there is a contract or provision for the provision of data acquisition services,
- data acquisition services are the subject of a tender,
- there is one or more suppliers in the supply chain.

This Technical Specification does not apply to the provision of legacy datasets or 'off-the-shelf' products if there is no further data production or updating activities to manage. The final standard in this series of standards addressing climate change issues is the Technical Specification ISO/TS 14,092 (ISO/TS 14,092:2020(E)), which sets out adaptation planning requirements and guidelines for local authorities and communities. This document supports local authorities and communities in adapting to climate change based on vulnerability, impact and risk assessments. It also supports, in cooperation with relevant stakeholders, the prioritization and the development and subsequent update of the adaptation plan.

The scopes of the described standards related to addressing the issue of climate change multidimensionally meet the needs of researchers and practitioners in the search for space to create effective solutions that can be implemented in economic practice and addressing the issue of the quality of life of citizens. They are a very important area of knowledge that can be successfully used as guidelines for creating practical solutions and conducting research that changes the principles of understanding environmental issues and enforcing new laws describing these problems. Based on their content, digital platforms can be created and hybrid and digital business models can be commercialized and implemented in business practice. Based on their assumptions, it is possible to search for new spaces for technological revolutions in the area of climate change.

4.7 Conclusions

A proper understanding of the logic, methodology and conceptual frame of the energy transformation opens an amazing and innovative direction for the development of business, the economy and society. The individual needs of global and local communities can be combined with institutional needs by creating coherent energy needs. Both the resource nature of energy and its structure adjusted to economic and technological expectations offer multidimensional values that should be noticed and skillfully used. A well-defined and economically understandable energy mix should be a tool for meeting the energy expectations of communities and a platform for improving the quality of their lives.

References

Barabino, E., Fioriti, D., Guerrazzi, E., Mariuzzo, I., Poli, D., Raugi, M., Razaei, E., Schito, E., & Thomopulos, D. (2023). Energy communities: A review on trends, energy system modelling, business models, and optimisation objectives. *Sustainable Energy, Grids and Networks, 36*, Article 101187. https://doi.org/10.1016/j.segan.2023.101187

Becker, S., Frew, B. A., Andresen, G. B., Zeyer, T., Schramm, S., Greiner, M., & Jacobson, M. Z. (2014). Features of a fully renewable US electricity system: Optimized mixes of wind and solar PV and transmission grid extensions. *Energy, 72*, 443–458. https://doi.org/10.1016/j.energy.2014.05.067

ERA Industrial Technology Roadmap. (2022, March). For low-carbon technologies in energy-intensive industries, European Commission, 1st edition. https://doi.org/10.2777/92567, European Union, 2022.

Erdiwansyah, et al. (2021). *Protection and Control of Modern Power Systems, 6*, 3. https://doi.org/10.1186/s41601-021-00181-3
Gitelman, L., & Kozhevnikov, M. (2023). New business models in the energy sector in the context of revolutionary transformations. *Sustainability, 15*, 3604. https://doi.org/10.3390/su15043604
https://www.pcbc.gov.pl/pl/blog/certyfikacja/zmiany-klimatu-a-wymagania-iso-9001 [dostęp: 19.01.2025].
International Standard ISO 14090, Adaptation to climate change—Principles, requirements, Reference number ISO 14090:2019(E).
International Standard ISO 14091, Adaptation to climate change—Guidelines on vulnerability, impacts and risk assessment, Reference number ISO 14091:2021(E).
International Standard ISO 14093, Mechanism for financing local adaptation to climate change — Performance-based climate resilience grants — Requirements and guidelines, Reference number ISO 14093:2022(E).
International Standard ISO 14097, Greenhouse gas management and related activities—Framework including principles and requirements for assessing and reporting investments and financing activities related to climate change, Reference number ISO 14097:2021(E).
International Standard ISO 19115–1, Geographic information — Metadata — Part 1: Fundamentals, Reference number ISO 19115–1:2014(E).
International Standard ISO 19115–2, Geographic information — Metadata — Part 2: Extensions for acquisition and processing, Reference number ISO 19115–2:2019(E).
International Standard ISO 19131, Geographic information — Data product specifications, Reference number ISO 19131:2022(E).
International Standard ISO 19156, Geographic information — Observations, measurements and samples, Reference number ISO 19156:2023(E).
International Standard ISO 19157, Geographic information—Data quality, Reference number
International Standard ISO 32210, Sustainable finance—Guidance on the application of sustainability principles for organizations in the financial sector, Reference number ISO 32210:2022(E).
ISO 19157:2013(E).
ISO 9001:2015 Quality management systems—Requirements, Published (Edition 5, 2015), This publication was last reviewed and confirmed in 2021.
Ji L., Huang X. (2022). Analysis of social governance in energy-oriented cities based on artificial intelligence, *Energy Reports 8*,11151–11160, https://doi.org/10.1016/j.egyr.2022.08.206.

Jurasz, J., Canales, F. A., Kies, A., Guezgouz, M., & Beluco, A. (2020). A review on the complementarity of renewable energy sources: Concept, metrics, application and future research directions. *Solar Energy, 195*, 703–724. https://doi.org/10.1016/j.solener.2019.11.087

Małek, A., Marciniak, A., & Bednarczyk, T. (2024). Probabilistic analysis of electricity production from a photovoltaic–wind energy mix for sustainable transport needs. *Sustainability, 16*, 10164. https://doi.org/10.3390/su16231 0164

Rinne, M. (2004). Technology roadmaps: Infrastructure for innovation. *Technological Forecasting &Social Change, 71.*

Ringkjøb, H. K., Haugan, P. M., & Solbrekke, I. M. (2018). A review of modelling tools for energy and electricity systems with large shares of variable renewables. *Renewable and Sustainable Energy Reviews, 96*, 440–459. https://doi.org/10.1016/j.rser.2018.08.002

Technical Specification ISO/TS 14092, Adaptation to climate change—Requirements and guidance on adaptation planning for local governments and communities, Reference number ISO/TS 14092:2020(E).

Technical Specification ISO/TS 19158, Geographic information—Quality assurance of data supply, Reference number ISO/TS 19158:2012(E).

Technology Roadmap. (2010, October). Carbon capture and storage, IEA Publications, 9 rue de la Fédération, 75739 Paris Cedex 15, Printed in France by Corlet.

Weitemeyer, S., Kleinhans, D., Vogt, T., & Agert, C. (2015). Integration of Renewable Energy Sources in future power systems: The role of storage. *Renewable Energy, 75*, 14–20. https://doi.org/10.1016/j.renene.2014.09.028

CHAPTER 5

Systematic Literature Review—A Description of the Landscape of Research Into Harnessing the Technological Revolution in the Fight Against Climate Change in the Context of the Functions of Digital Business Models

Abstract The aim of this chapter is to present the results of a systematic literature review in relation to a description of the landscape of research into harnessing the technological revolution in the fight against climate change in the context of the functions of digital business models. The scope of the chapter covers issues related to the sources of the technological revolution in the fight against climate change in the context of the functions of digital business models. The subject of the chapter concerns a multidimensional cognitive perspective aimed at shaping the principles governing the factors influencing the technological revolution in the fight against climate change in the context of the functions of digital business models in relation to both theoretical cognition and implementation aspects.

Keywords Systematic literature review · Landscape of research · Multidimensional cognitive perspective · Theoretical cognition and Implementation aspects

A. Jabłoński and M. Jabłoński, *Digital Business Models and Environmental Action*,
https://doi.org/10.1007/978-3-032-15298-5_5

5.1 Introduction

The aim of this chapter is to present the results of a systematic literature review in relation to a description of the landscape of research into harnessing the technological revolution in the fight against climate change in the context of the functions of digital business models.

The scope of the chapter covers issues related to the sources of the technological revolution in the fight against climate change in the context of the functions of digital business models.

The subject of the chapter concerns a multidimensional cognitive perspective aimed at shaping the principles governing the factors influencing the technological revolution in the fight against climate change in the context of the functions of digital business models in relation to both theoretical cognition and implementation aspects.

5.2 A Description of the Landscape of Research into Harnessing the Technological Revolution in the Fight Against Climate Change in the Context of the Functions of Digital Business Models

For the purpose of scientific research into the relationship of the technological revolution to reversing the climate change process in the context of the determinants of the creation of digital business models, a study was conducted by means of a method of a systematic literature review. Scientific articles and grey literature were used. In order to be able to properly understand the principles of harnessing the technological revolution in the fight against climate change, it is important to conduct a professional process related to this systematic literature review in order to obtain the appropriate characteristics of the landscape of research into the factors affecting the technological revolution.

In the course of scientific discussion, two research hypotheses were formulated in this context:

> Hypothesis 1: The technological revolution strengthens the fight against climate change through environmental action.
> Hypothesis 2: The functions of digital business models influence the fight against climate change.

The following describes the scope and subject of research which aimed to verify hypothesis 1, namely that the technological revolution strengthens the fight against climate change.

In the relevant literature, the concept of technological revolution, together with the concept of climate change, is thoroughly characterized and described. The same is true for digital business models and climate change. The objective of the systematic literature review on technological revolution and climate change in the context of environmental action and digital business models is to examine whether it is based on scientific evidence. For the purpose of conducting a systematic literature review, a review of the potential combinations of compiled search terms was used, namely:

- Digital Business Models AND Environmental Action.

The Scopus and Web of Science databases were used. The following results were obtained in this regard: Scopus—100 articles, WoS—212 articles. A total of 48 duplicates were also received. Based on the research, a suitable Prisma model was developed for the terms of Digital Business Models AND Environmental Action. Figure 5.1 shows the Prisma model developed for these terms:

For articles that were included, a semantic map of key concepts was prepared. The minimum number of occurrences of a keyword was set at five. Out of 761 keywords, 17 met the threshold.

Table 5.1 provides a list of identified keywords related to the terms 'digital business models' and 'environmental action.'

A detailed distribution of acquired concepts and their relationships is presented in the semantic map developed in VOSviewer, a software tool for constructing and visualizing bibliometric networks. These networks may include, for example, journals, researchers or individual publications, and may be constructed on the basis of citation, bibliographical coupling, co-citation or co-authorship relationships. VOSviewer also offers a text mining functionality that can be used to construct and visualize networks of co-occurrence of important terms extracted from scientific literature [https://www.vosviewer.com/] (Fig. 5.2).

As above, a systematic literature review was conducted on the basis of an earlier review of potential combinations of compiled search terms, namely: 'technological' and 'revolution' and 'climate' and 'change'

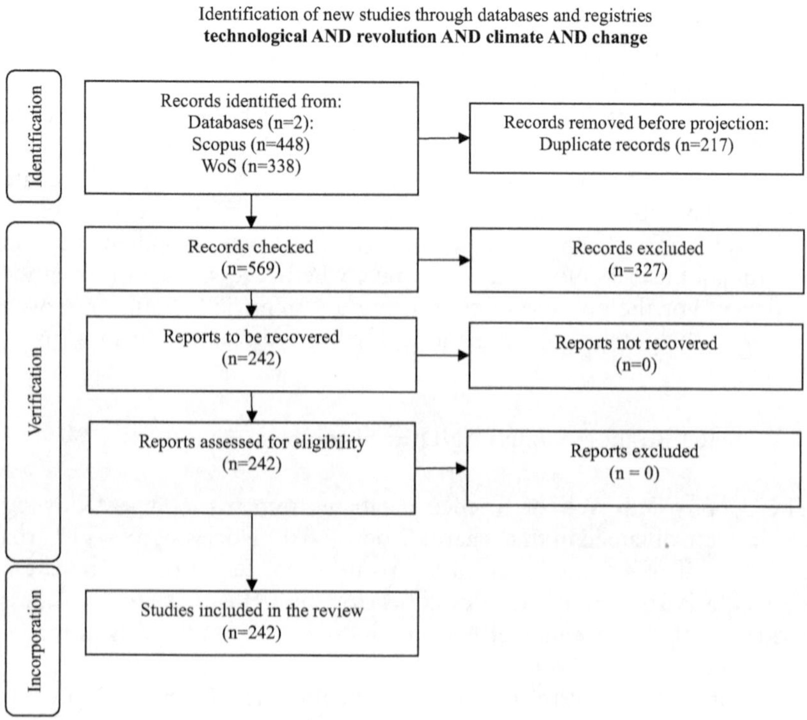

Fig. 5.1 The Prisma model for the terms: Digital business models and environmental action (*Source* Own study)

Scopus and Web of Science databases were used. The following results were obtained in this regard: Scopus—448 articles, WoS—338 articles. A total of 214 duplicates were also received.

Based on the research, the Prisma model was developed for the terms 'technological' and 'revolution' and 'climate' and 'change.'

Figure 5.3 shows the Prisma model developed for these terms.

For articles that were included, a semantic map of key concepts was prepared. The minimum number of occurrences of a keyword was set at five. Out of the 1738 keywords, 43 met the threshold.

Table 5.2 provides a lists of the keywords identified for the terms 'technological' and 'revolution' and 'climate' and 'change.'

Table 5.1 List of identified keywords for the terms: Digital business models AND environmental action

Id	*Keyword*	*Occurrences*	*Total link strength*
59	blockchain	5	8
66	business	5	9
72	business models	7	9
98	circular economy	16	22
105	climate change	5	4
188	digital storage	5	4
196	digital transformation	7	11
199	digitalization	5	15
241	energy	5	6
364	impact	9	12
383	innovation	7	11
429	management	10	18
465	models	5	6
510	performance	5	8
669	sustainability	16	27
678	sustainable development	9	13
680	sustainable development goals	6	3

Source Own study

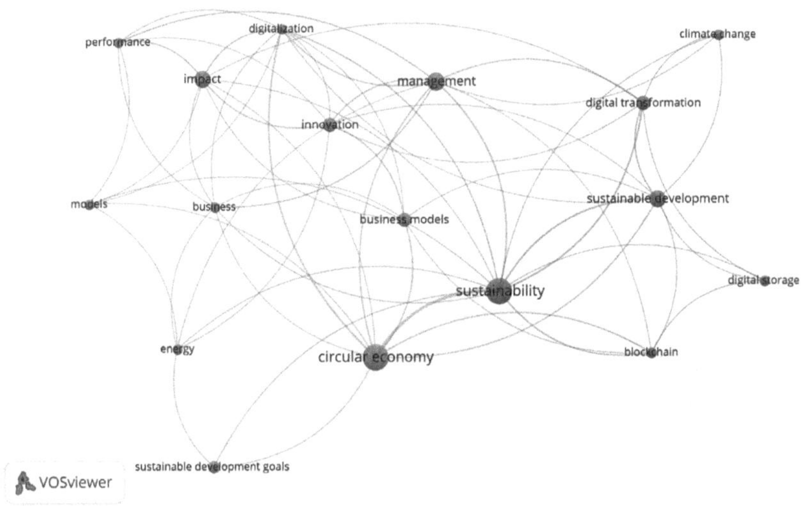

Fig. 5.2 The semantic map of key concepts for the terms: Digital business models and environmental action developed in VOSviewer (*Source* Own study)

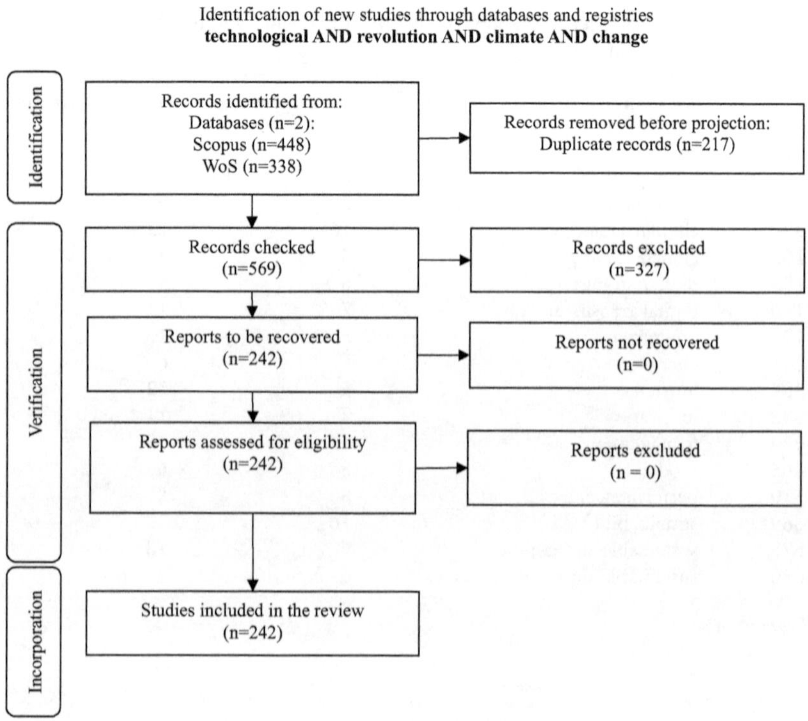

Fig. 5.3 The Prisma model for the terms: technological AND revolution AND climate AND change (*Source* Own study)

A detailed distribution of acquired concepts and their relationships is presented in the semantic map developed in VOSviewer, a software tool for constructing and visualizing bibliometric networks. These networks may include, for example, journals, researchers or individual publications, and may be constructed on the basis of citation, bibliographical coupling, co-citation or co-authorship relationships. VOSviewer also offers a text mining functionality that can be used to construct and visualize networks of co-occurrence of important terms extracted from scientific literature [https://www.vosviewer.com/] (Fig. 5.4).

The research based on the methodology of the systematic literature review has shown that both the relationship between the technological revolution and its impact on the better fight against climate change

Table 5.2 List of identified keywords for the terms: Technological AND revolution AND climate AND change

Id	*keyword*	*Occurrences*	*Total link strength*
19	adaptation	7	18
43	agriculture	10	23
121	big data	6	10
144	biotechnology	5	9
166	carbon	8	23
170	carbon dioxide	8	22
183	carbon neutrality	6	9
203	challenges	5	11
211	china	11	23
227	climate	8	20
228	climate change	61	121
239	climate-change	15	25
246	co_2 emissions	7	16
452	economic growth	6	10
456	economic-growth	6	15
473	efficiency	6	10
494	emissions	7	20
503	energy	18	52
534	energy transition	13	22
632	food security	10	29
651	fossil fuels	5	14
652	fourth industrial revolution	8	14
674	future	8	25
728	global warming	13	35
756	green revolution	9	24
760	greenhouse gases	7	20
771	growth	8	17
845	impact	11	29
847	impacts	8	20
863	industrial revolution	5	10
864	industrial revolutions	5	12
877	industry 5.0	5	8
889	innovation	12	22
1172	performance	6	12
1231	power	5	5
1320	renewable energy	7	14
1537	sustainability	22	53
1547	sustainable development	17	44
1567	systems	7	24

(continued)

Table 5.2 (continued)

Id	*keyword*	*Occurrences*	*Total link strength*
1587	technological innovation	8	19
1590	technological revolution	5	13
1595	technology	7	21
1699	water	5	13

Source Own study

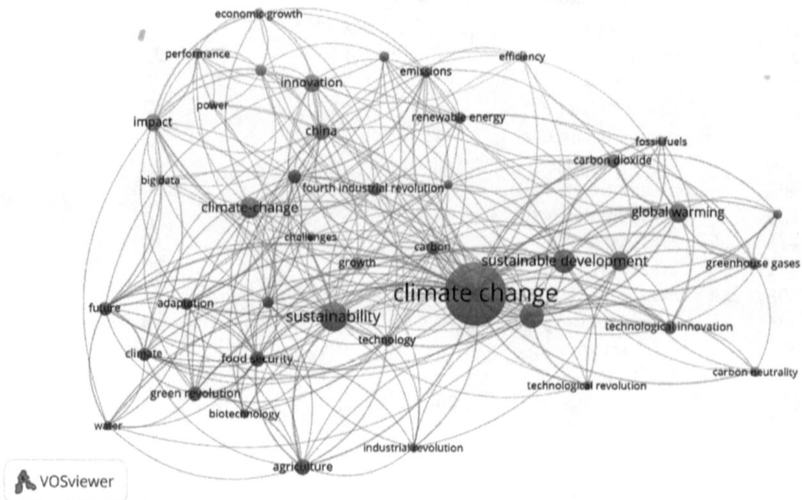

Fig. 5.4 The semantic map of key concepts for the terms: Technological AND revolution AND climate AND change developed in VOSviewer (*Source* Own study)

through environmental action and the functions of digital business models and their impact on the fight against climate change are hot topics in the world literature. Both of these terms generate a very large number of scientific publications related to numerous new ontological concepts which are important for the development of this subject, indicated on semantic maps created in the course of research.

5.3 Conclusions

A systematic literature review of the theoretical and practical approach to the issue of the technological revolution in the context of climate change, taking into account environmental action as well as digital business models and climate change, is fundamental to understanding its place and role in the business, economic and social existence of companies and other types of organizations and people in the rapidly deepening climate crisis. Understanding these relationships against the background of climate change at the level of world literature allows for a multi-criteria assessment of these relationships.

A systematic literature review is crucial to determining the relationship between the studied concepts for scientific cognition. The proper selection of keywords and their importance and significance open the way to understanding the very essence of the climate problem as well as extracting proposals for a strategic and tactical–operational decision-making process for it. Knowledge and science always create a special platform for proper substantive reasoning and correctly implemented inferences.

CHAPTER 6

Technological and Organizational Revolution Towards Positive Climate Change

Abstract The aim of this chapter is to present technological and organizational revolution towards positive climate change. The revolution in business, the economy and society is complex and can have numerous dimensions and pillars. The core dimensions and pillars are technological, organizational and economic ones. In order for climate systems to fully fulfil their role, they must be based on logical substantive assumptions strongly embedded in scientific solutions. Smart climate systems should meet the criteria for their safe integration and technical compatibility. Algorithmic thinking plays an important role in climate change management processes. Algorithmic thinking is the ability to approach specific problems in a systematic and structured way, similar to the operation of an algorithm in a computer. This consists primarily of breaking down complex problems into smaller, more manageable steps, identifying appropriate patterns and creating more effective solutions. The theory of constraints can be a strategic methodology for climate governance mechanisms.

Keywords Technological and organizational revolution · Positive climate change · Economy and society · Algorithmic thinking

A. Jabłoński and M. Jabłoński, *Digital Business Models and Environmental Action*,
https://doi.org/10.1007/978-3-032-15298-5_6

6.1 Introduction

The revolution in business, the economy and society is complex and can have numerous dimensions and pillars. The core dimensions and pillars are technological, organizational and economic ones. In order for climate systems to fully fulfill their role, they must be based on logical substantive assumptions strongly embedded in scientific solutions. Smart climate systems should meet the criteria for their safe integration and technical compatibility. Algorithmic thinking plays an important role in climate change management processes. Algorithmic thinking is the ability to approach specific problems in a systematic and structured way, similar to the operation of an algorithm in a computer. This consists primarily of breaking down complex problems into smaller, more manageable steps, identifying appropriate patterns and creating more effective solutions. The theory of constraints can be a strategic methodology for climate governance mechanisms. The assumption that the functioning of any system can be described by an algorithm of a defined chain of events or a network composed of chains is crucial to the theory of constraints (Goldratt, 1990, p. 53).

6.2 Architecture of Dynamic Climate Systems in Climate Change Adaptation Processes

Climate systems have a component structure that targets an aggregated set of these components as a function of the objective of positive climate adaptation at the levels of the region, city and company. The concept of Event-Driven Architecture (EDA) applies here. EDA has emerged as a promising architecture for the development of distributed systems, with promising gains in modularization, scalability and concurrency (Cao et al., 2020). EDA is often adopted in applications for handling large amounts of data in continuous streams (Fertier et al., 2020).

Event-Driven Architecture, also known as EDA, is an architectural model that assumes that detection, generation and reaction to events are the main elements controlling the flow through the system. In EDA, events are generated based on the state of the application or system and then transmitted to the relevant system components that are responsible for processing these events. This approach allows for the creation of scalable, highly reactive and flexible systems that are capable of processing large amounts of data and events in real time. In particular, EDA is used in distributed systems, systems supporting transactions or in the so-called Big Data systems, where the ability to quickly respond to changes in the state of the system is the key to improving the quality of customer service, optimizing efficiency and effectiveness or increasing security.

Figure 6.1 shows the dynamic climate adaptation demonstrated in a stratified system.

The model of climate adaptation presented in Fig. 6.1 has the character of a dynamic layered system, where changes pass from above to lower levels of social life functioning. Change processes are cascaded from the level of the world affected by cosmic space to regions, cities and even businesses. In this way, the system is fully airtight and affects all areas of social life in the world. Climate events, regardless of the level at which they occur, affect the full system, whether in the top-down or bottom-up direction. Everywhere there is a change that needs to be addressed through climate change management systems. Big Data and information collected at all levels of the system are used for decision-making. The scalability and concurrency of the system are important. These two features allow for

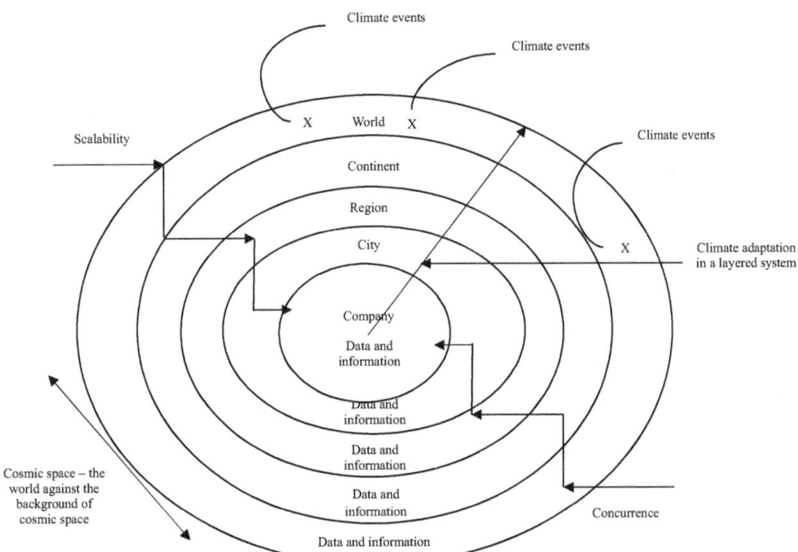

Fig. 6.1 Dynamic climate adaptation demonstrated in a stratified system (*Source* Own study)

the development of flexible adaptation strategies to climate change at all levels of the system. The skillful management of climate change in climate adaptation processes is a core determinant of achieving an acceptable level of climate transition. Climate change can be technical, operational and organizational. Climate change in socio-economic ecosystems is both negative and positive. The economics of climate change in economic and social processes is very important for the function of all human existential functions (Stern, 2007). The mechanisms adopted for the effective and efficient management of climate change can be implemented in an evolutionary and revolutionary way.

6.3 Industry 4.0 and 5.0 Solutions—Smart Manufacturing Focused on Environmental and Climate Issues

The concepts of Industry 4.0 and Industry 5.0 are an important and progressive element in the development of production systems. The solutions used therein are also focused on carbon footprint minimization issues that support the processes of reducing the negative impact on climate change. Eco-friendly and smart manufacturing is a key challenge for modern factories. The implementation of production based on innovative strategies and pro-ecological technologies allows manufacturing companies to optimize costs, improve the effectiveness and efficiency of processes and consequently optimize and reconfigure the value chain, often towards the circular economy. There is, therefore, a need for such an approach to the organization of production that is conducive to eliminating the adverse impact on climate change. Modern societies are forcing increased awareness among product manufacturers and service providers of the approach to stopping negative climate change, which in recent years has been manifesting in a number of negative weather phenomena and affecting the earth's ecosystem. The requirements of sustainability-focused customers are aimed at this, so companies have to take into account ecological criteria, including in the assessment of the course of processes (Bergs et al., 2020, p. 488). Configurations of business models of manufacturing enterprises should be based on solutions and technologies which are in turn based on the assumptions of the circular economy. Investments in organic production, maintenance and exploitation throughout the life cycle of a product and service should translate into a reduced price of products with unimpaired product quality and a high level of greening. Such greening should apply to the entire production system. The number of adverse factors influencing environmental pollution should be eliminated. The concept of green production is also based on the optimization of the value chain, including in particular the lean manufacturing method. Positive effects related to the increased carbon footprint also include the selection of ecological materials, manufacturing technologies, the course of production processes and even assembly techniques. Production management to neutralize climate change can occur if product and process innovation is directed to reducing the environmental impact and bettering it when it contributes to beneficial climate impacts. Manufacturers can optimize manufacturing processes based on resource consumption and process improvement, and innovate to manage material and energy consumption to link environmental impacts to the product produced. In production, a digital twin solution can also be used to collect ecological information and convert it into impact variables (Lürken et al., 2023, pp. 62–367). In enterprises using innovative environmental monitoring systems in real time, it is possible to record environmental data throughout the entire production process. It is also important to capture the correlation between the different factors of production in order to achieve so-called green productivity in the production process (Zhao& Lyu, 2024). The leading trends in the relationship between the industrial revolution in production and climate change are the concepts of the blue economy, green production and green conservation. The blue economy is a continuation of the green economy. It is based on the creation of innovative processes for the use of waste treated as raw materials in iteratively implemented cycles based on biological processes naturally occurring in nature. Green production plays an important role in optimal energy consumption, reducing emissions to soil and air, developing a recycling economy and building a resource-saving and environmentally friendly society (Kadhum & Hameed, 2023, pp. 82–97). One cannot endlessly strive for an exponential increase in resource consumption to last indefinitely. In such an approach, sustainable technologies should be selected at the early stages of the exploitation of technical and organizational systems. In many situations, the principles of green preservation are applied, which is based on the following (Ajukumar & Gandhi, 2013, pp. 34–46): reducing problems caused by leakages, reducing problems related to waste disposal operations, reducing adverse environmental impacts by adopting effective waste treatment rules, encouraging organizations to use environmentally friendly maintenance materials such as lubricating oils and cleaning materials, maintaining the health and safety of workers by reducing risks related to maintenance operations and the use of non-toxic materials, using modern digital technologies in the maintenance process and moving away from traditional maintenance, using energy-efficient materials and maintenance equipment.

6.4 Simulations and Digital Twins and the Internet of Things in the Process of Searching for Innovative Mechanisms of Impact on Climate Change

The development of digital simulations is an important link in creating innovative solutions in the area of predictive processes detecting weak signals of change. The concept of digital twins is based on the identification of a process that is subject to the mapping of reality for the purpose of streamlining, introducing changes, detecting weaknesses and indicating potential changes for the real system. It consists of presenting such scenarios of system operation that could not be implemented in real conditions or the costs of such analysis would be extremely high. The digital twin is developed for a specific purpose, e.g., the optimization of system performance parameters, control-oriented applications, monitoring and the management cockpit (Ali et al., 2024). The digital twin is a virtual replica of robots that allows for real-time monitoring, analysis and simulation of their activities and environment. Sensors on robots collect data from the physical world, including information pertaining to location, obstacles and environmental conditions. The communication network facilitates the exchange of data between robots and their digital twins, enabling seamless real-time communication. The flow of data from physical robots to the digital twin provides key information for decision-making and control (Rahmani et al., 2024, p. 8). Advances in machine learning, the Internet of Things (IoT) and Big Data have led to significant improvements in digital twin features such as real-time monitoring and accurate forecasting. Despite this progress and the efforts of individual companies, there are some gaps in research and implementation in this area that have so far prevented the widespread adoption of digital twin concepts and technologies (Sharma et al., 2022, p. 9).

Digital twins, the virtual representations of physical entities, can model and predict the behavior of materials, enabling improved design, testing and fabrication of materials. However, the comprehensive use of digital twins for predictive analysis and process optimization in materials science remains largely unexplored. Digital twins are virtual replicas of physical entities that replicate real-time behavior, and have emerged as a breakthrough technology with enormous potential in materials science (Tur, 2023, pp. 172–190). Domains of digital transformation and digital twins explore their important roles in shaping the factory of the future. At the heart of this transformation lies the Internet of Things (IoT) and the Industrial Internet of Things (IIoT), offering a channel for the introduction of the circular economy (CE). However, the advent of the Green Internet of Things paradigm, focused on energy reduction and the carbon footprint, is juxtaposed with the advent of Artificial Edge Intelligence (AI). Industry 5.0 represents the subsequent phase of production evolution, combining automation with a human factor, human needs and limitations (Rahmani et al., 2024, p. 787). Digital twin applications are evolving exponentially and changing the way companies operate. Over the past few years, digital twins have leveraged core business applications, and the technology is expected to expand to more applications, use cases and industries. In recent years, the concept has been defined, the evolution and development of digital twins have been highlighted, its key enabling technologies have been discussed and its trends, challenges and applications in various industries have been explored (Attaran & Gokhan Celik, 2023). Recently, the popularity of simulation-based solutions using simulators operating offline or online with access to real-world data, as in the case of digital twins, has been growing significantly. Since the issues of the climate and climate change are not obvious and unambiguous, the only effective way to imagine the state of the future environmental ecosystem is the use of digital economy solutions and the technology of predictive detection of potential changes. Combining the needs for the implementation of climate services, understood as actions aimed at detecting and responding to potential trends of change through a system of alerts or actions reducing the risk of negative scenarios in this area, the need arises to seek the possibility of predicting changes. Therefore, simulating the situation of various weather anomalies or climate change in this natural area is possible only through the use of digital economy solutions. Reality mapping requires the determination and conducting of the simulation based on specific conditions and adopted assessment criteria. Innovative mechanisms of impact on climate change can also be sought by means of the Internet of Things, which allows for communication between things and interactions to perform specific activities without human intervention. This understanding of reality is conducive to the creation of technical systems that provide a framework for the automation and robotization of industrial processes. The focus on climate change and environmental protection is associated with the implementation of numerous iterations that allow for the development of possible scenarios that can provide information to researchers in this field. The use of digital twins in the process of mapping climate change against unexpected weather anomalies poses a strong challenge and can be said to be the natural working environment of digital twins. Supporting these processes with the Internet of Things can contribute to solutions based on the predictive detection of weak signals, testing scenarios that are worrying in terms of weather and climate risks, which should consequently influence the best preparation of protective weather changes in order to develop effective and efficient solutions based on early warning systems against adverse events in the context of conditioning climate change. The modern concepts of the digital economy have a significant impact on the development of pro-ecological management issues, especially in the context of identifying such factors that have an impact on climate change. Rationalizing this approach, this is not only about maximizing actions and directions to neutralize climate change, but doing it in such a way as not to harm the development of the world's economies. This development should be balanced and based on a pragmatic approach allowing the achievement of business goals including the creation of profits, but also ensuring the conditions of the quality of life of the inhabitants of the earth, balance in this area, social justice and the development of the value economy based on an understanding of the desires, expectations and requirements of a wide variety of stakeholder groups. For modern concepts of the digital economy to develop in a sustainable way, they must be based on clear and international law-compliant premises that do not contradict each other. Such a modern approach to business promotes universal social acceptance and enables managers to create a business culture based on care for the well-being of employees' lives and work. Conscious good decision-making, i.e., that does not generate conflicts and does not exploit the weak, is a challenge for the modern economy. Modern technologies are intended not only to serve global corporations, which through their dominant positions can dictate conditions to others, but also to enable the development of smaller enterprises, which may have something to offer that a large player may not pay attention to. The creation of revolutionary solutions does not belong only to large players, as evidenced by the great successes of some startups that can undermine the rules of the game in the sector and become so-called game changers. The ability to think creatively and come up with new ideas is proof of freedom, efficiency of thinking and creating new spaces depending on market position, place of business location, nation, access to modern technologies or financial limitations. Even these important factors do not have to be a barrier to creating innovative solutions that change the conditions of the game in the sector and even in the entire economy. The freedom of creation, the ability to break rules and create new paradigms not only depends on strong scientific centers, but can be conducive to production even by small enterprises, whose flexibility and lack of administrative burden can be an advantage. The ability to detect weak signals based on the prediction of future needs depends on the determination of creators and certain specific attributes that, under certain conditions, can unleash unexpected ideas that, through conceptualization and operationalization, can be successfully implemented into business practice and, at the same time, create the foundations for new scientific theories. The relationship between science and business in the context of the conditions for the creation of new functions and performance of digital business models may materialize in the form of implementations, patents and licenses. In today's business world, the development of solutions with a high level of market attractiveness is often conditioned by luck and speed of entering the market. Timing is also important, i.e., the moment when a given product or service can achieve spectacular success. Therefore, most actions that managers take today are based on the creation of new technologies that undermine the current status and violate the rules of business. It can be stated that the ability to break the rules is inherent in every man who will unleash the capability of doing so within himself. Rule breaking may have both regional and transnational character. Figure 6.2 shows the determinants of change in thinking for the purpose of searching for breakthroughs in understanding the impact of climate change on natural, social and business ecosystems.

Technological empiricism is not a naturally blind wavering from one ill-considered experiment to another. The inventor of the practices has a

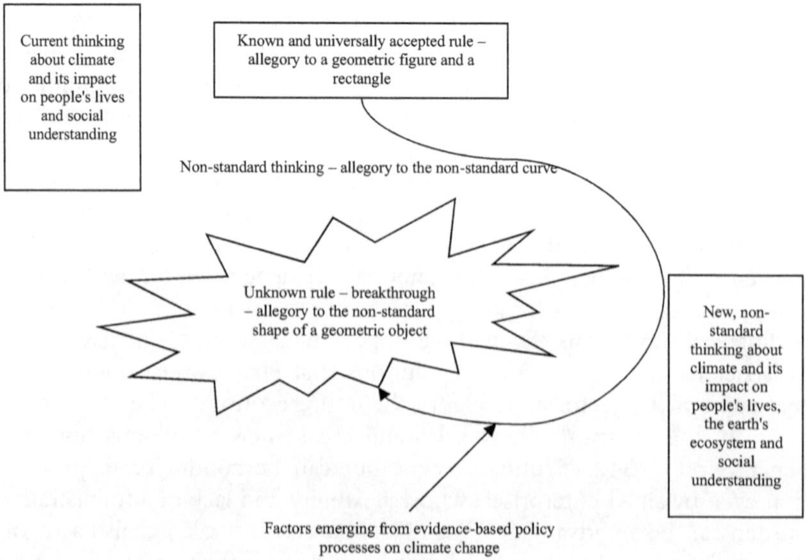

Fig. 6.2 Determinants of changes in thinking for the purpose of searching for breakthroughs in understanding the impact of climate change on natural, social and business ecosystems (*Source* Own study)

concept, or rather, thanks to what he has already done (or what others have done before him), he sees a small piece in front of him (Lem, 2020, p. 39). This is proven by the success of companies such as Apple, Meta (formerly Facebook), Amazon, Elon Musk's projects and other examples of global success for players in the digital economy.

6.5 Assumptions for the Design, Development and Management of Predictive Systems in the Operation, Organization and Maintenance of Socio-Technical Systems

The technological revolution linked to technological progress in the field of environmental protection, especially in the context of climate change neutralization, can be examined from numerous perspectives. One such perspective is the inclusion of solutions based on predictive maintenance processes of production systems and subsystems in the production system. Reducing the number of failures and ensuring the continuity of the system makes the consumption of energy, material resources, human resources and other factors affect the potential loss of production reduce the impact on the environment. Changes in the configuration of production systems and logistics systems, especially in the area of process optimization, taking into account cost time and quality, significantly affect ecological aspects. The ability to reconfigure these processes for ecological optimization is an important topic for system designers who want to achieve results enabling them to compete with other solutions through the price criterion. The parallelism of price optimization through technological progress is conducive to gaining a competitive advantage based on technology. Integration processes of ecological aspects with predictive maintenance experience require intelligent transformational change processes in production systems focused on the goal of balancing environmental impacts. Theoretical models of ecological predictive maintenance emphasize the dynamic management of production systems, focusing on minimizing the impact on the environment while increasing the productivity, effectiveness and efficiency of the management of organic time, material and information resources. Improving production processes based on the assumptions of the circular economy is often supported by additional solutions based on the use of the assumptions of the Industry 4.0 concept, including digital twins, the Internet of Things or artificial intelligence. Thus, an innovative carrier of activities supporting ecological optimization processes for creating solutions conducive to reversing adverse climate change is generated. Modern electronic systems can be used to model changes in production systems through knowledge acquired during their observation and monitoring from many different perspectives, including operational, reliability, quality and ecological parameters. Ecologically-focused predictive maintenance enables the creation of mitigation potential, enabling producers to support a sustainable future while increasing the efficiency of processes to meet the high expectations of consumers regarding the mechanisms of production and service activities responsible for the environment. Organic production plays a fundamental role, particularly in cost aspects, in optimizing energy consumption, reducing emissions, promoting a recycling economy and supporting a resource-efficient and environmentally friendly society. It must be remembered that the resources released into the ecosystem then become waste. This ensures that the ecological factors embedded in the processes make it possible to change the attitude of manufacturing companies and transform linear supply chains belonging to traditional solutions into those based on the assumptions of the circular economy. Many authors are searching for a new approach to reducing emissions in maintenance processes. Applications of different approaches in this regard can be evaluated and optimized according to the ecological predictive maintenance approach (Simões et al., 2009). The idea of predictive maintenance fits into the aspects of climate change neutralization. Predictive maintenance predicts failures before they occur, based on random data collected continuously by machine sensors. Unlike reactive or programmable maintenance, which is triggered when a problem has already occurred or according to a set schedule, predictive maintenance uses advanced analytics to improve operational efficiency (Hosni, 2025, pp. 376–382). Advanced technology enables predictive maintenance that can be applied across industries, using Big Data analytics, smart sensors, artificial intelligence and platform construction. Such predictive quality management systems can become living ecosystems that can perform cause-and-effect analysis, Big Data monitoring and analysis and effective real-time decision-making. Ecological criteria must also play a crucial role in relation to legal and technological requirements, including in terms of optimizing production and service processes in a pro-ecological perspective. In this approach, the assumptions for a socio-technical system are important, which is based on the leading role of technology in relation to human activities as an operator who expects automated systems to carry out planned tasks using smart solutions often based on artificial intelligence, which support maintenance and operational processes and ensure the ability to achieve the intended goal. The function of the objectives in such systems is to maintain a high level of quality of these processes as well as to ensure a minimal impact on the environment. The intelligence of such solutions is therefore included in the basic understanding of ecological quality conditioned by modern technologies, data transmission of information and interfaces between complex technical systems characterized by specific, expected functions and performances.

6.6 Dynamic Capabilities in the Digital Revolution of Companies Based on Innovative Ecological Business Models

The concept of dynamic capabilities was developed in the United States (Teece et al., 1997, pp. 509–533) and aimed to neutralize the weaknesses of the Resource-Based View concept (Barney, 1991, pp. 99–120). The core idea behind this concept was for organizations to be flexible in using the resources needed to gain a competitive advantage. Dynamic capabilities maximize competitive forces through resource mobility. The key in this respect is technological resources that, together with organizational capabilities, create effective mechanisms of competition. Emphasizing the functioning in a turbulent environment requires searching for dynamic capabilities and the use of technology which is difficult to imitate and knowledge. In this approach, technology is the core resource of winning in the market. This concept fits perfectly into the assumptions of shaping business models based on technologies utilizing their revolutionary character in the era of widespread digital transformation. The capabilities in this management solution are conducive to configuring and reconfiguring internal and external competences for adapting the organization in a changing environment. Competences in this approach serve the effective use of technologies that are embedded in process structures and management systems. Dynamic capabilities are aimed at renewing competences for adaptation to a changing environment. Therefore, we are dealing with a combination of effective uses of technology thanks to our competences in a changing business environment. When we add the current conditions for the development of technologies that sell the creation of innovative, ecological business models focused on climate change to this, then this concept takes a new look at these topics. From this perspective, dynamic capabilities can indicate managers' responses to climate hazards and their consequences in the context of competitors' actions, which serve the resilience of the organization. The ability to make resources redundant, renew them and use them in different contexts proves the effectiveness of using dynamic capabilities. Then, regardless of the actions of competitors and their resources, the innovative technologies used can change the rules of the game in sectors and dynamize the company's ability to achieve a competitive advantage. Linking the dynamic capabilities of processes embedded in the structure of the business model can let these capabilities introduce new conditions for configuring resources and operating procedures. The greening of business processes can significantly accelerate the companies' transformation towards creating potential that is not easy for competitors to copy. Since dynamic abilities originate from within the organization, the essence of technological thinking and engineering understanding of management processes, the simple actions of competitors may not be effective in neutralizing this advantage. Certain organizational habits, which are often also called dynamic capabilities supported by business technology, will be very difficult for competitors to copy. If these dynamic capabilities of organizations rely on innovative green technologies and build the logic of the business model on them, the process of shaping dynamic capabilities can become a tool for accelerating the organization on the path to technological development. Digital economy solutions and a strong emphasis on the integration of processes to make changes in the organization will help reconfigure the ability to compete dynamically. This configuration and reconfiguration of resources in order to renew the vitality of the company determines the effectiveness of the implementation of the strategy of value creation. The technological revolution in the area of ecological criteria and the social acceptance of these activities, and even their coercion by society, may allow companies focused on such an understanding of functioning in a competitive market to achieve successes and long-term value increases. The reconfiguration of the value chain towards the circular economy can help boost the growth of technology-based companies. This approach fits into the contemporary paradigm of creating value through the use of revolutionary technologies, especially in the area of environmental protection, climate change monitoring services and the adaptation of business solutions to the expectations of the broadly understood society.

6.7 Intelligent Support Systems for Creating Climate Services That Monitor Climate Anomalies and Dysfunctions

Intelligent systems for the productive monitoring of climatic anomalies and dysfunctions are developing in the form of pro-climate services. These services are used to detect early signals of potential adverse impacts on the environment, weather changes, unnatural behaviors, unnatural behaviors of natural ecosystems, changes in vegetation processes, carbon dioxide impacts, changes in watercourses and a number of other variables that can be monitored. In this regard, digital technologies in particular have the potential to be used for the development of early warning systems coupled with variable monitoring processes based on Big Data, which, through the exchange of data and the interaction between them, enable the creation of crisis management systems that meet the contemporary needs of responding to current threats. An overview of the key definitions of climate services is presented in Table 6.1.

The intelligence built into these services helps show how wide this cognitive area is and how many more areas should be covered by these activities. This is a very broad area of prospects for the development of this type of service, which, in principle, should be included in normal operational management in every part of the lives of citizens and the functioning of businesses. Only through a wide range of such services is it possible to systemically capture all potential anomalies with a unified surveillance system that will warn institutions and citizens against irresponsible calculations in the face of climate and weather threats. Such smart support systems are based on digital smart innovative technologies that very often break the rules of the game in sectors, as they are based on new scientific paradigms and are often even pre-paradigmatic. The aim of these services is to introduce preventive systems in the first place, and if they are based on sensors, predictive systems that detect threats, risks and initiate the implementation of appropriate risk control measures for a given situation and neutralize any shift in its effects.

6.8 Conclusions

Adaptation to climate change should have a systemic dimension. The complexity of this issue requires such causal thinking and action that should translate into a far-reaching stream of positive results in the area of climate protection. The approach to these issues should focus on both technical and organizational aspects. The integration of these climate actions can create new concepts, techniques and management methods and link them to novel and innovative technological processes. Then, so-called technical organizations will become a certain factor in the creation of socio-technical systems for the generation of positive climate change.

Table 6.1 Overview of key definitions of climate services

No	*Definition of climate service*	*Core attribute definition*
	Transformation of climate-related data, together with other relevant information, into tailor-made products such as projections, information, trends, economic analyses, assessments (including technological ones), advice on best practices, the development and assessment of solutions and any other climate-related services that may be useful to the general public European Commission (2022)	Data transformation, best practices, useful for society
	Climate services are defined by the 'WMO Global Framework for Climate Services' as 'providing climate information in such a way as to aid decision-making' Hewitt et al. (2012)	Information, decision-making
	Definition of Climate Europe: 'Climate service is the provision of climate information to assist decision-making. The service must respond to user needs, must be based on scientifically credible information and expertise, and requires appropriate engagement between the users and providers' Climateurope (2020)	Information, decision-making, user needs
	Climate services can be seen as a form of sustainable innovation that 'takes into account environmental, social and economic considerations in their development and use' Larson (2007)	Sustainable innovation, development, use
	Climate services are a specific type of knowledge-based activity, knowledge-intensive business services (KIBS), i.e., characterized by non-financial services requiring a high level of knowledge due to the high density of human capital Brenner et al. (2017)	Knowledge, non-financial services
	These services are designed to facilitate climate adaptation, disaster risk mitigation and reduction, which are widely recognized as important sustainability challenges in both rich and poor countries Asrar et al. (2012)	Climate adaptation, disaster risk, sustainability

(continued)

Table 6.1 (continued)

No	*Definition of climate service*	*Core attribute definition*
	Climate services include those features that incorporate them into business models Larosa and Perrels (2017)	Functions, business models
	Climate services can be defined as decision support tools developed based on the process of transforming climate information into appropriate advisory services that assist in decision-making by individuals and social organizations. The climate service provides tailored, relevant and useful advice to policymakers and vulnerable communities, based on available climate information (for example, forecasts). The service requires an appropriate involvement in the creation of advice relevant to the user's needs, to assist him/her in making decisions in conditions of uncertainty and to facilitate and set the direction of early action and readiness. The service also means the effectiveness of the access and delivery mechanism. First of all, a climate service responding to the needs of users is necessary Tall and Njinga (2013)	Decision-making, climate information transformation, advisory services
	Climate services embody the production, explanation and transfer of climate research into useful information for climate-related decision-making Vaughan et al. (2018)	Production, research transfer, decision-making

Source Jabłoński (2023, p. 140)

References

Ajukumar, V. N., & Gandhi, O. P. (2013). Evaluation of green maintenance initiatives in design and development of mechanical systems using an integrated approach. *Journal of Cleaner Production, 51*, 34–46.

Ali, Z., Biglari, R., Denil, J., Mertens, J., Poursoltan, M., & Kaba Traor M. (2024). From modeling and simulation to digital twin: Evolution or revolution? Article in simulation: Transactions of the society for modeling and simulation international, 3.

Asrar G.R., Ryabinin V., Detemmerman V. (2012), Climate science and services: Providing climate information for adaptation, sustainable development and risk management, *Current Opinion in Environmental Sustainability*, 4(1), pp. 88–100.

Attaran, M., & Gokhan Celik, B. (2023). Digital twin: Benefits, use cases, challenges, and opportunities. *Decision Analytics Journal, 6*, Article 100165.

Barney, J. (1991). Firm resources and sustained competitive advantage. *Journal of Management, 17*(1), 99–120.

Bergs, T., Grünebaum, T., Rey, J., Barth, S., & Goldmanns, M. (2020). A methodology for the ecological and economic assessment of manufacturing process sequences. *Procedia CIRP, 90*, 488.

Brenner T., Capasso M., Duschl M., Frenken K., Treibich T. (2017), Causal relations between knowledge-intensive business services and regional employment growth, *Regional Studies*, 52(2), pp.172–183.

Cao, H., Yang, X., & Deng, R. (2020). Ontology based holonic event-driven architecture for autonomous networked manufacturing systems. *IEEE Transactions on Automation Science and Engineering, 18*(1), 205–215.

ERA Industrial Technology Roadmap. (2022, March). ERA industrial technology roadmap for low-carbon technologies in energy-intensive industries, European Commission, 1st edition. https://doi.org/10.2777/92567, European Union, 2022,

Fertier, A., Montarnal, A., Barthe-Delanoë, A.-M., Truptil, S., & Bénaben, F. (2020). Real-time data exploitation supported by model-and event-driven architecture to enhance situation awareness, application to crisis management. *Enterprise Information Systems, 14*(6), 769–796.

Goldratt, E. M. (1990). *The haystack syndrome: Sifting information out of the data ocean* (p. 53). The North River Press.

Hewitt, C., Mason, S., & Walland, D. (2012). The global framework for climate services. *Nature Climate Change*, 2, 831–832, climateurope | Linking science and society

Hosni H. (2025). Predictive maintenance in the era of industry 5.0: Challenges and opportunities. *Journal of Materials and Engineering, 03*(4)376–382.

Jabłoński, A. (2023). Usługi klimatyczne w kształtowaniu modeli biznesu przedsiębiorstw [Climate services in shaping business models of companies]. Przegląd Organizacji.

Kadhum, A. A. L., & Hameed, H. A. (2023). The effect of green maintenance on environmental performance applied research in the general company for oil products. *Management and Production Engineering Review, 14*(3), 82–97.

Larson, B. A. (2007). *Sustainable development research advances*. Nova Publishers

Larosa F., & Perrels A. (2017). *Assessment of the existing resourcing and quality assurance of current climate services, Grant agreement 730500, EU MACS European Market for Climate Services, Deliverable 1.2.*

Lem, S. (2020). *Summa Technologiae* (p. 39). Wydawnictwo Literackie.

Lürken, C., Grünert, G., Stauder, L., Barth, S., & Bergs, T. (2023). Concept for life cycle oriented ecological assessment in tooling. *Procedia CIRP, 120*(3), 62–367.

Rahmani, R., Jesus, C., & Lopes, S. I. (2024). Implementations of digital transformation and digital twins: Exploring the factory of the future. *Processes, 12*(4), 787.

Sharma, A., Kosasih, E., Zhang, J., Brintrup, A., & Calinescu, A. (2022). Digital twins: State of the art theory and practice, challenges, and open research questions. *Journal of Industrial Information Integration, 30*, 9.

Simões, A., Farinha, T., Fonseca, I., Barbosa, F. M., & Marques V. (2009). Buses degradation based on exploration conditions. In *Proceedings of the 3rd WSEAS Int. Conf. on Energy Planning, Energy Saving, Environmental Education.*

Stern, N. (2007). *The economics of climate change (the stern review).* Cambridge University Press.

Tall A., & Njinga J. (2013). *Developing a methodology to evaluate climate services for farmers in Africa and South Asia workshop report, CGIAR Program on Climate Change, Copenhagen, Denmark, Agriculture and Food Security.* https://org.www.www.ccafs.cgiar

Teece, D. J., Pisano, G., & Shuen, A. (1997). Dynamic capabilities and strategic management. *Strategic Management Journal, 18*, 509–533.

Tur, E. (2023). Harnessing the power of digital twins for enhanced material behavior prediction and manufacturing process optimization in materials engineering. *Bayburt University Journal of Science, 6*(2), 172–190.

Vaughan C., Dessai S., Hewitt C. (2018), Surveying climate services: what can we learn from a bird's eye view?, *Weather, Climate, and Society*, 10(2), pp. 373–395.

Zhao, J., & Lyu, Y. (2024). Research on intelligent green manufacturing process monitoring based on target detection and environmental monitoring technology. *Thermal Science and Engineering Progress, 53*, Article 102766.

CHAPTER 7

Adaptation to Climate Change in Terms of Organizational Revolutions

Abstract The aim of this chapter is to present the core principles of adaptation to climate change against the background of the organizational revolution of companies, cities and regions. Adaptation to climate change is a broad process of adapting natural, social and economic systems to the current or anticipated impacts of climate change, with the aim of limiting harm and harnessing potential benefits. The scope of the chapter covers the issues of strategic management of climate knowledge and the principles of climate engineering in shaping new organizational solutions. It also covers areas of disinformation and destabilization in the area of climate science, including against the background of crises of a proper understanding of global warming and other climate factors. The subject of the chapter is to explain the mechanisms of climate adaptation in the area of knowledge management, climate engineering, strategic management of regions and cities and disinformation and climate destabilization.

Keywords Adaptation to climate change · Organizational revolutions · Climate knowledge · Climate engineering

A. Jabłoński and M. Jabłoński, *Digital Business Models and Environmental Action*,
https://doi.org/10.1007/978-3-032-15298-5_7

7.1 Introduction

The aim of this chapter is to present the core principles of adaptation to climate change against the background of the organizational revolution of companies, cities and regions. Adaptation to climate change is a broad process of adapting natural, social and economic systems to the current or anticipated impacts of climate change, with the aim of limiting harm and harnessing potential benefits. The scope of the chapter covers the issues of strategic management of climate knowledge and the principles of climate engineering in shaping new organizational solutions. It also covers areas of disinformation and destabilization in the area of climate science, including against the background of crises of a proper understanding of global warming and other climate factors. The subject of the chapter is to explain the mechanisms of climate adaptation in the area of knowledge management, climate engineering, strategic management of regions and cities and disinformation and climate destabilization.

7.2 Strategic Management of Climate Knowledge Versus the Development of Climate Responsibility

Knowledge is always essential for adopting the appropriate and correct interpretation of data and information in a difficult communication space, and is required everywhere. Knowledge effectively eliminates populism and a pathological understanding and representation of reality. It should be developed in all possible places and dimensions. It should reach out with truth to every member of the current humanity, especially if it concerns such an area of human existence, which can be the source of various processes of the nature of manipulation and disinformation, including infodemics. Knowledge is understood here as the appropriate use of information and data in a given context and with understanding. Climate knowledge management is a very important component in shaping and developing climate responsibility. This applies to organizational, managerial and technological knowledge. Climate knowledge management should serve to develop climate capital within the organization both at the level of individuals, i.e., personnel within the organization, and at the institutional level, i.e., the entire organization. Climate knowledge management should be supported by the development of other types of capital, taking into account adopted and well-informed climate criteria. This type of capital will certainly include organizational capital, innovative capital, relational capital and human capital. Human capital is particularly important here, insofar as it can be examined from the perspective of a key resource of the organization, and then the concept of human resource management can be used. In economic terms, the concept of human capital and, from the humanism-oriented perspective, people management can be used. With regard to knowledge management, climate knowledge is also explicit and implicit, as is the case with other types of knowledge. However, it should be remembered that due to the permanent development of a negative attitude to climate change in various environments resulting from, among others, populist behavior, individuals may be aware of the climate problem, but hide this fact due to possible threats to their personal security. Hence, ignorance or falsehoods resulting from the infodemic often arise. Figure 7.1 shows the forces of socio-political attraction against the background of development and society's awareness of climate change.

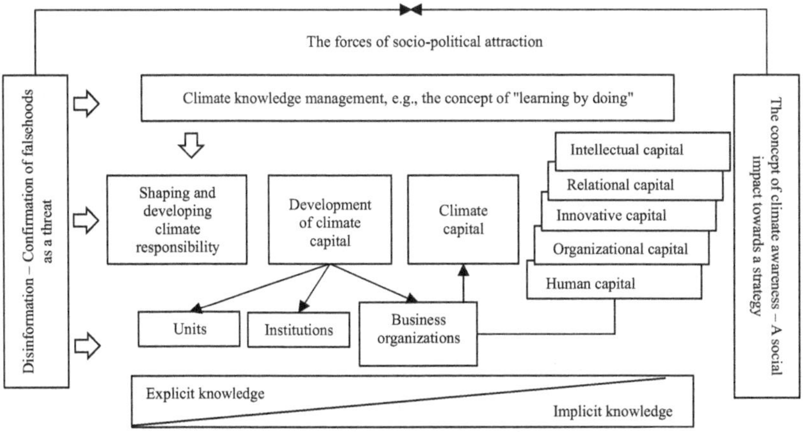

Fig. 7.1 The forces of socio-political attraction against the background of development and awareness of societies about climate change (*Source* Own study)

7.3 Strategic Management of Climate Responsibility-Oriented Regions and Cities

The region and the city are two very important entities that are directly and indirectly affected by climate change. The local community often bears huge personal costs, and the social and economic region in the case of a high frequency of occurring anomalies and climate dysfunctions, not to mention climate catastrophes. The area-based, point-based nature of cities and regions is important for the management of climate responsibility mechanisms, especially in strategic terms and above all because it is precisely in these cities and regions that anomalies, dysfunctions and climate extremes occur. Climate change not only relates to increased temperature, but also changes in, among others, precipitation, air humidity, wind strength and the occurrence of snow cover, which affect the occurrence of species of flora and fauna in a given ecosystem. A region and a city can be considered an aggregated area-based system with the feedback loops defined therein. For this reason, cities and regions should be strongly strategically oriented towards the principles of climate responsibility and focused on the broad shaping thereof in the key decision-making links creating climate policy. The climate policies of cities and regions should ensure that they have adequate climate resilience. Climate resilience should be assessed and verified by the criterion of its effectiveness (Li & Duan, 2005). In fact, two concepts related to this can be defined here. On the one hand, it will be climate resistance, i.e., the ability to protect against dynamic climate change. However, in an interpretation with a greater climate impact, the concept of climate resilience may apply. The climate resilience of a region or city can be defined as the ability to maintain comprehensive climate protection while ensuring the capacity for sustainable development at the level of various existential factors conditioned by the specific operating criteria of the region or city. It should be borne in mind that dynamic urbanization, worrying demographic changes, social changes, the development of innovation and digital technologies and climate change particularly determine the logically justified development of regions and cities. The concept of urban resilience, i.e., the concept of resilient cities, applies here. Urban resilience is characterized by the ability of the urban system and all its components to maintain or rapidly recover from the functions concerned in the face of disruptions; adapting to change and being able to rapidly transform the system; and an ability to avoid and manage threats (Bosher & Coaffee,

2008). Urban resilience refers to the ability of an urban system—and all its constituent socio-ecological and socio-technical networks across temporal and spatial scales—to maintain or rapidly return to typical functions in the face of a disturbance, to adapt to change and to quickly transform systems that limit current or future adaptive capacity (Meerow et al., 2016, pp. 183–193). Figure 7.2 shows the factors determining the emergence of strategies for cities/regions to respond to climate change by developing resistance and resilience plans.

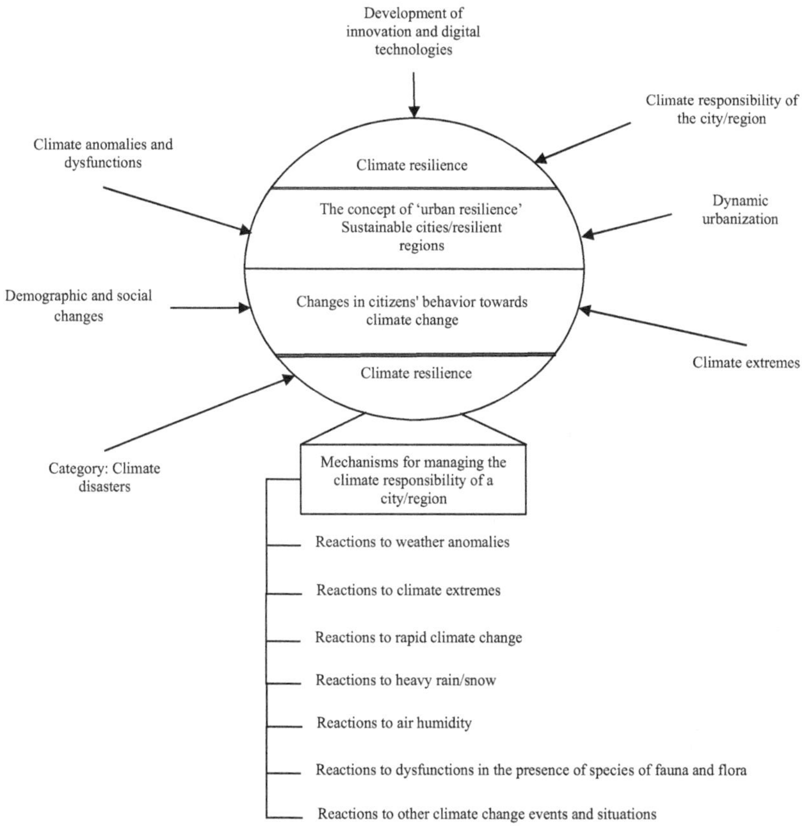

Fig. 7.2 Factors determining the formation of strategies for the response of cities/regions to climate change by developing climate resilience and resilience plans (*Source* Own study)

According to such logic of perceiving the city and the region, a stream of opportunities and benefits occurs that change the perception of them as adverse to the climate and thus definitely improve the quality of life therein. In addition, the logic of managing the region and the city is implemented according to the principles of the 'Smart City' and 'NetZeroCities' concepts. The Smart City concept moves towards the concept of a sustainable city, where resource savings concern not only the environmental aspect, but also economic, social and spatial aspects in the context of the functioning of a region or city. The NetZeroCities concept aims to drastically reduce greenhouse gas emissions in regions and cities through climate action to achieve climate neutrality. Adaptation to the climate and its positive change becomes a decisive factor in choosing the place of residence and shaping the existential functioning of people in given cities and regions. Positive climatic attributes are and will continue to be a factor in choosing the place of residence.

7.4 The Difference Between Global Warming and Climate Change and the Climate Adaptation of Businesses

A great number of people do not believe in global warming, which is a huge global problem. All this should be explained in great detail by means of various types of communication solutions. There is a fundamental difference between global warming and climate change. The Fifth Assessment Report of the Intergovernmental Panel on Climate Change (IPCC, 2013) was announced in 2013. It revealed that climate change is undeniable and scientifically proven and can be attributed to human activity with 95% probability, which unfortunately is not understood by a wide group of people subjected to information manipulation. In global warming, the greenhouse effect associated with dynamically increasing concentrations of gases such as CO_2, CH_4, N_2O and dust in the atmosphere is largely significant. In order to maintain the level of use of these gases, it is necessary to constantly invest. The greenhouse effect is a natural phenomenon that can lead to life on Earth. An important difference between global warming and climate change arises. Global warming means a steady and systematic increase in the global average air temperature over a certain observation period. The main reason for the acceleration of these changes is the strong interference with natural ecosystems and direct human

Table 7.1 List of selected effects of global warming

No	*Selected effects of global warming*
1.	Melting of natural ice and glaciers
2.	Sea and ocean level rise
3.	Increased frequency and intensity of extreme weather events
4.	Disturbances of the water cycle in nature
5.	Extending the vegetation period of flora
6.	The steppe-formation process of areas hitherto covered with regular vegetation and increased frequency and extent of forest fires
7.	Changes in the range of species of flora and fauna, including pests and vectors of infectious diseases

Source Own study

activity, which has led to a significant increase in the temperature of land, oceans and the atmosphere. The directly visible effects of global warming include those listed in Table 7.1.

Climate change is severely affecting existing natural ecosystems and systems of human existence in different regions of the world. One of the biggest impacts of climate change directly affects changing biodiversity. Ecosystems are constantly disturbed by rising air temperatures, changing rainfall patterns and retreating glaciers. Many species of animals and birds are unable to adapt to these changes, which results in the extinction thereof and loss of biodiversity. In addition, habitat fragmentation is a major problem hindering the mobility and reproduction of different species. In different ecosystems, agriculture is one of the most vulnerable sectors to climate change. Expanding droughts in many parts of the world and rising high temperatures strongly affect agricultural yields. They also cause large water shortages for soil irrigation and increase the spread of various pest groups. It also has a direct impact on the availability of drinking water, causing health problems and the spread of various types of diseases. Building stable systems that restore natural states to their original state is a much-needed dedicated action to stop these processes. Nature Restoration Law means restoring weakened or damaged ecosystems by improving their structure and functions, with the overall aim of increasing the resilience and biodiversity of natural resources. In the European Union, this is done through the implementation of the Regulation of the National Plan for the Reconstruction of Natural Resources.

7.5 Disinformation and Destabilization in the Area of Climatology as a Strategic Threat in the Climate Adaptation Processes of Companies

Real information, data and knowledge hold the greatest intellectual potential for various forms and formulas of human, economic and social activity. The introduction of false information into the system of interpersonal communication is a great strategic threat in various perceptual dimensions in relation to the reality around us. The formulation of fiction is often difficult to discover, and the systematic creation of this fiction can also become an element of warfare, military activities of hostile states or communities, including terrorist ones. Looking in detail at social communication systems on a global scale, we can say that we are currently dealing with a pandemic of disinformation in the area of climatology. There is a kind of infodemic here in the full sense of the word. The term 'infodemic'—a portmanteau of the words 'information' and 'epidemic'—was created to outline the dangers of disinformation, speculation and gossip, amplified and rapidly spread around the world, mainly by means of modern communication technologies (Zarocostas, 2020). This is reflected in the approach to climate change.

Climate responsibility should be based on sound scientific results—scientific evidence. There are many theories denying science in favor of pseudoscience, rubbish, nonsense, the description of miracles and common nonsense in public space. Science should not give in to questioning the basic facts and fight for the truth, as depicted in Fig. 7.3.

The concept of disinformation in the current situation of global conflict is fundamental from the perspective of the so-called cognitive cyber warfare. Disinformation is an extremely powerful weapon in the hands of war aggressors and digital hackers. Cognitive warfare is treated as a convergence of information warfare, intelligence, surveillance and reconnaissance, electronic warfare, psychological operations and cyber operations, using digital and network infrastructure. It may also cover the scopes of climatology, interpreting it, for example, as so-called predatory climateism and, on the basis of such rhetoric, the pursuit to provoking permanent conflicts that cause, for example, social mutual aggression, which may even lead to violent aggression. Such actions can be triggered and implemented by so-called climate deniers. One should be aware that in cognitive warfare, the human mind becomes a battlefield and it is the target of attack. In order to win this war, one must first win the battle for

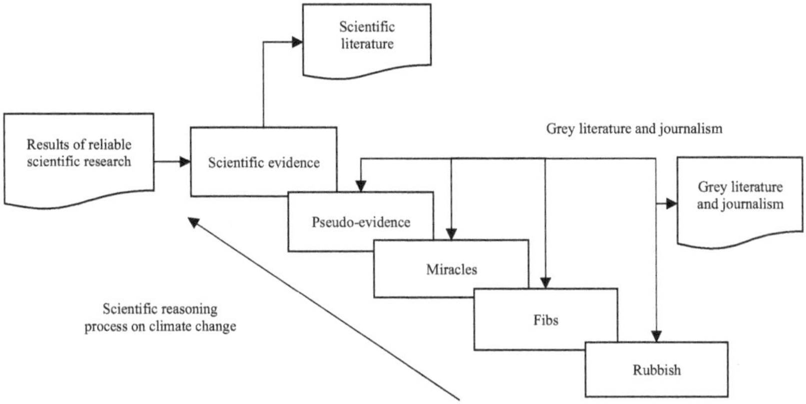

Fig. 7.3 Evolution of the search for scientific evidence in the process of confirming climate change (*Source* Own study)

public opinion. Winning must then be achieved by scientific argumentation based on facts and evidence. Considering climate disinformation widely, Climate Action Against Disinformation (CAAD) [https://caad.info/] draws attention to the following features of disinformation:

- undermining the existence of and unequivocal human impact on climate change and the need for appropriate and urgent action in line with the scientific consensus of the IPCC and the objectives of the Paris Agreement on Climate Change;
- misrepresentation of scientific data, including cherry-picking, to undermine trust in climate institutions, experts and solutions;
- publicizing false actions as supporting climate goals that actually contribute to climate warming or contradict the scientific consensus on climate change mitigation or adaptation. As a result, unfortunately, such actions cause an uncontrolled negative discourse on real climate change, which causes delays in real climate change. Scientists see this very dangerous phenomenon resulting from climate disinformation and try to prevent or reduce it, despite the fact that in many cases systemic adaptation to climate change is delayed. A strong threat to climate action is the spread of fake news. Social media is widely used here, creating manipulative actions against the online community (Mashamaite, pp. 183–193). In this approach and

interpretation, climate disinformation is a hugely negative factor in shaping the principles of climate responsibility among various social groups, business and the economy.

For example, artificial intelligence can generate disinformation. It can not only generate content, but also manipulate various images; one such technique is the so-called deepfake, which is combining and applying still and moving images to other images or videos using deep learning algorithms (Cole, 2018). Dystopia can be a source and platform of inspiration for the use of disinformation. Dystopia (from the ancient Greek δυσ (dus) 'bad' and τόπος (tópos) 'place'), also called cacotopia or anti-utopia, is a community or society that is extremely bad or frightening (Merriam-Webster, 2012; Rüsen et al., 2005). All of this can cause multidimensional social instability as a result of failure to maintain the right level of climate security. A very important element required to be covered by professional legal solutions is so-called paid disinformation. All mechanisms of neutralizing this pathological phenomenon should be implemented, which also affects the processes of positive climate change. Climate security is fleeting, impermanent, unstable, labile, and creates a great variety of problems of the nature of internal and external order. The stabilizing part of the climate security system is the appropriate organizational structure and its skillful use at the level of the country, the region, the city or the company; however, different circumstances of climate security are changeable.

7.6 Conclusions

A suitable approach, understanding and interpretation of adaptation to climate change determines the appropriate decision-making systems not only in the area of the climate, but in fact in every component of the business and social existence of companies, regions and cities. Such an interpretive perspective becomes a platform for planning, organizing, controlling and motivating at the level of various types of entities. At the same time, in order to implement appropriate milestones for this adaptation, increasing disinformation and destabilization related to the understanding—or lack thereof—of climate change must be eliminated. Therefore, the generator of the right approach to these difficult issues should be the proper use of climate knowledge and climate engineering solutions.

References

Bosher, L., & Coaffee, N. (2008). Editorial: International perspective on urban resilience, urban design and planning, 161, nr DP4. climatique basées sur la performance — Exigences et lignes directrices.

Cole, S. (2018). *We are truly fucked: Everyone is making AI-Generated fake porn now*. Vice.com. https://www.vice.com/en/article/bjye8a/reddit-fake-porn-app-daisy-ridle

https://caad.info/

International Standard ISO 14090 First edition (2019–06). *Adaptation to climate change—Principles, requirements and guidelines* [Adaptation au changement climatique — Principes, exigences et lignes directrices].

International Standard ISO 14091 First edition (2021–02). *Adaptation to climate change—Guidelines on vulnerability, impacts and risk assessment* [Adaptation au changement climatique — Lignes directrices sur la vulnérabilité, les impacts et l'évaluation des risques].

International Standard ISO 14093 First edition (2022–1). *Mechanism for financing local adaptation to climate change—Performance-based climate resilience grants: Requirements and guidelines* [Mécanisme pour le financement de l'adaptation au changement climatique à l'échelle locale — Subventions pour la resilience].

International Standard ISO 14097 First edition (2021–05). *Greenhouse gas management and related activities—Framework including principles and requirements for assessing and reporting investments and financing activities related to climate change* [Gestion des gaz à effet de serre et activités associées — Cadre comprenant les principes et les exigences pour l'évaluation et la déclaration des investissements et des activités de financement au regard du changement climatique].

International Standard ISO 19115–1 First edition (2014–04–01). *Geographic information—Metadata—Part 1: Fundamentals* [Information géographique — Métadonnées — Partie 1: Principes de base].

International Standard ISO 19115–2 Second edition (2019–01). *Geographic information—Metadata—Part 2: Extensions for acquisition and processing* [Information géographique — Métadonnées — Partie 2: Extensions pour l'acquisition et le traitement].

International Standard ISO 19131 Second edition (2022–11). *Geographic information—Data product specifications* [Information géographique — Spécifications de contenu informationnel].

International Standard ISO 19156 Second edition (2023–04). *Geographic information—Observations, measurements and samples* [Information géographique — Observations, mesures et échantillons].

International Standard ISO 19157 First edition (2013–12–15). *Geographic information—Data quality* [Information géographique — Qualité des données].

International Standard ISO 32210 First edition (2022–10). *Sustainable finance—Guidance on the application of sustainability principles for organizations in the financial sector* [Finance durable — Lignes directrices pour l'application des principes de durabilité aux organisations dans le domaine financier].

Intergovernmental Panel on Climate Change - IPCC, 2013

Li, G., & Duan, H. (2005). Robustness assessment of climate policies towards carbon neutrality: A DRO-IAMS approach. *Computers & Operations Research, 174*, Article 106879. https://doi.org/10.1016/j.cor.2024.106879

Mashamaite, M. M. The Impact of Misinformation and Fake News on Climate Change Perception and Response: A Comprehensive Review. *International Journal of Social Science Research and Review, 6*(9), 183–193.

Meerow, S., Newell, J. P., & Stults, M. (2016). Defining urban resilience: A review. *Landscape and Urban Planning, 147*, 38–49. https://doi.org/10.1016/j.landurbplan.2015.11.011

Merriam-Webster. (2012). *"Definition of "dystopia""*. Oxford Dictionaries. Oxford University Press.

Rüsen, J., Fehr, M., & Rieger, T. (2005). *Thinking Utopia: Steps into other worlds*. Berghahn Books. ISBN 978-1-57181-440-1.

Technical Specification ISO/TS 14092 Reference number ISO/TS 14092:2020(E) First edition (2020–05). *Adaptation to climate change—Requirements and guidance on adaptation planning for local governments and communities* [Adaptation au changement climatique — Exigences et recommandations relatives à la planification de l'adaptation pour les autorités locales et les communautés].

Technical SpecificatiON ISO/TS 19158 First edition (2012–10–15). *Geographic information—Quality assurance of data supply* [Information géographique — Assurance qualité relative à l'approvisionnement de données].

Zarocostas, J. (2020). How to fight an infodemic. *The Lancet, 395*(10225), 676.

CHAPTER 8

Accelerators of Dynamic Processes of the Technological and Digital Revolution in the Context of Climate Change Determinants

Abstract The aim of this chapter is to present accelerators of dynamic processes of the technological and digital revolution in the context of climate change determinants. In order to be able to effectively and efficiently design and implement the principle of technological and digital revolution in the context of the determinants of climate change, a very important element of this process is the search for appropriate driving factors, which can be called carriers of technological and digital values for the climate. An appropriate accelerator can serve this purpose, understood as a mechanism, tool or institution that accelerates the creation of economic, social or technological value. There is a need for such dynamics in this space, which will inhibit the rapidly advancing climate crisis and its adverse impact on the existence of humanity in various fields of its functioning. Such an approach determines the speed of changes taking place and will also reduce the level of frustration of global and local communities related to anomalies, dysfunctions and climate catastrophes. As such, great determination and creativity of innovators and decision-makers in various fields and mechanisms of climate governance is required.

Keywords Accelerators of dynamic processes · Technological and digital revolution · Climate change determinants · Social or technological value

A. Jabłoński and M. Jabłoński, *Digital Business Models and Environmental Action*,
https://doi.org/10.1007/978-3-032-15298-5_8

8.1 Introduction

In order to be able to effectively and efficiently design and implement the principle of technological and digital revolution in the context of the determinants of climate change, a very important element of this process is the search for appropriate driving factors, which can be called carriers of technological and digital values for the climate. An appropriate accelerator can serve this purpose, understood as a mechanism, tool or institution that accelerates the creation of economic, social or technological value. There is a need for such dynamics in this space, which will inhibit the rapidly advancing climate crisis and its adverse impact on the existence of humanity in various fields of its functioning. Such an approach determines the speed of changes taking place and will also reduce the level of frustration of global and local communities related to anomalies, dysfunctions and climate catastrophes. As such, great determination and creativity of innovators and decision-makers in various fields and mechanisms of climate governance is required.

8.2 Factors Determining the Impact of the Technological Revolution on the Success of Companies—the Principles of the Implementation of Innovative Green Solutions—Creative Destruction

Technological progress caused by innovation changes the rules of the game in the space of life and business. Creative destruction is particularly important in areas related to environmental protection, including climate change issues. Societies are increasingly influencing the external environment by forcing political, social and economic action, which should be conducive to reducing the adverse impact on climate change. Industrial age technologies should be replaced by digital economy solutions with a positive environmental impact. The dynamics of development and technological progress are increasingly exponential, which proves the rapid pace of implementation of innovation. New products and services are created as a result of value-creating business models. Solutions to halt adverse climate change are related in particular to the digital transformation, the greening of business processes, the development of new forms of energy generation and inventiveness, especially in the area of artificial intelligence. These are the factors that determine the impact of the technological revolution on the success of a company. The search for solutions conducive to halting climate change is not only economically justified from the perspective of potential market opportunities, but in particular has an impact on social expectations and the improvement of the quality of life of the earth's inhabitants. Every place in the world is searching for innovative solutions that are characterized by functionality focused on these aspects of business creation. Climate change monitoring technologies, the recipients of which are state institutions and business, play an important role in this respect. The examples of such solutions include satellite systems for monitoring climate change, the use of drones supported by artificial intelligence, as well as geolocation issues. These and other solutions support breakthroughs in progressive technological solutions. Modern technologies based on the assumptions of the digital economy are increasingly used in monitoring climate change. These include, but are not limited to, drones for data collection, IoT and sensors for data collection, Earth observation for planetary intelligence, artificial intelligence, AR/VR to visualize climate impacts and advanced computing to power intelligence (Innovation and Adaptation in the Climate Crisis 2024). This technological progress proves the great potential of this subject to create revolutionary solutions based on the network and system approach.

8.3 The Role of Satellite Monitoring Systems and Artificial Intelligence in the Area of Climate Change Measurement and Monitoring

Satellite-based climate change monitoring systems are crucial to identifying the current state of change and the possibility of neutralizing adverse factors. Studying climate variables is a difficult task because no technique can reliably generate the necessary data on both a small and large scale. However, the Earth Observation System and numerous proposed satellite systems enhance the assessment of significant climate variables (Omali, 2022, p. 15). New insights and analyses are made possible by the global and small-scale spatial range of satellite observations. By contrast, the short duration of the series of observations and their uncertainties continue to pose challenges for capturing the robust long-term trends of many climate variables (Yang et al., p. 875). Satellites provide a wealth of data critical to understanding the complexity of our planet's climate system, from tracking climate change to observing weather patterns and monitoring environmental phenomena. Satellites equipped with infrared sensors measure the temperature of the Earth's surface and the atmosphere, which helps observe temperature changes over time (Murphy, 2023, p. 1). The most important measurement variables include atmospheric composition, ocean surface topography, precipitation, land surface imaging, ocean color radiometry, an ocean surface wind vector and sea surface temperature (Dowell et al., 2013). The observed trends represent well-understood responses to global warming, in particular the widespread cooling of the lower stratosphere and warming of the troposphere (Gleisner et al., 2022, p. 1). The major tools used to monitor climate change are remote sensing, deep learning and computer vision systems (Gupta et al., 2022). Extensive information networks are essential for modern climate change monitoring. A network effect built with complex monitoring systems distributed in such a way as to ensure the best possible measurement capacity is necessary. Artificial intelligence solutions play a particular role in this regard. The ability to improve climate change monitoring systems is a prerequisite for better analysis of the factors responsible for the state of the climate.

8.4 Combining Drones as Physical Cyber Systems with Artificial Intelligence in Climate Change Monitoring

Climate change monitoring for natural ecosystems is studied on different spatial and temporal scales. Different observational and experimental approaches are used to identify trends, changes and for different ecological indicators (Díaz-Delgado et al., 2019, p. 64). In particular, drone technologies are becoming commonplace. Drones equipped with AI-based systems can facilitate the implementation of adaptive management strategies by providing timely and accurate information. With their help, it is possible to monitor changes in vegetation, water quality and wild animal populations. They underlie the construction of systems for building ecosystem resilience (Bekmurzaeva et al., 2024, p. 1). Drones are often used for climate-related research because they make it easier to monitor environmental changes over time in coastal areas, tropical forests, glaciers, wetlands and other remote places that are difficult to study due to difficult accessibility (Knight, 2022/2023, p. 8). Drones are equipped with technologies including propulsion systems, infrared cameras, GPS, navigation systems, programmable controllers and automatic flight planning with data processing software (Vikas et al., 2019, p. 74). They can also be used to map urban heat islands, assess the energy efficiency of buildings, monitor air quality and identify sources of greenhouse gas emissions (Bayomi & Fernandez, 2023, p. 1). In particular, artificial intelligence used in drone systems significantly supports the usefulness of the data obtained. Thus, drones can create physical cyber systems with artificial intelligence. In this form, they significantly strengthen the ability to monitor climate change.

8.5 Artificial Intelligence and Smart Geolocation Solutions. Application of Artificial Geospatial Intelligence (GeoAI) in Climate Adaptation Processes

Artificial intelligence is a fundamental factor responsible for the digital and technological revolution in business models. It stimulates new business models based on a technological approach. Artificial intelligence is unleashing new spaces of action and becoming an accelerator of the digital revolution. Taxonomies for identifying digital business models based on artificial intelligence are already emerging. An example is the taxonomy which consists of 11 dimensions and 39 characteristics and is based on the conceptual representation of the business model. Each combination of features in dimensions results in a new instance of the AI startup's business model. For example, for the value proposition area, the aspects of artificial intelligence are based on autonomous robots and bots, while in terms of value creation it will be robotics, visual data and mixed data. In the field of value delivery, operationalization can be carried out through AI-produced output. Finally, as regards value capture, it will be one-time payment (Weber et al., 2022, p. 98). Artificial intelligence directs its potential to transforming business models, taking into account the relationship between technological innovation and business strategy. Artificial intelligence needs to interact with different aspects of business, in the context of the role of artificial intelligence in business innovation to shape AI-driven business models. Since modern business must be supported by scientific solutions, the implications of AI solutions derived from scientific solutions for business cannot be overestimated in this respect, which strengthens the chances of creating progressive solutions that change the rules of the game in sectors and the economy (Bianchini et al., 2022, p. 1). In practice, for example, the use of artificial intelligence in creating business models can be based on the construction of AI business platform models, which is practically understood on an equal footing with the SaaS model in the cloud. This includes AI solutions that can work together on the top tier of other digital systems, such as customer relationship management (CRM) and enterprise resource planning (ERP) business systems (Mishra & Tripathi, 2021, p. 1). The frequent use of artificial intelligence in the design of business models sets new business opportunities for new companies, thus creating new cognitive spaces and market opportunities. It seems reasonable to formulate the statement that it is artificial intelligence that will become a revolutionary modern game changer against the background of designing and implementing new innovative business models. Artificial Geospatial Intelligence (GeoAI) is developing very dynamically in the context of climate change monitoring conditions and any processes supporting this topic. GeoAI can be used in various interesting application fields such as precision agriculture, environmental monitoring, disaster management and urban planning (Boutayeb et al., 2024, p. 1). The GeoAI framework can also be used to build a comprehensive Individual Tree Inventory and quantify the cooling of tree species under the influence of increasing urban heat (Das et al., 2022, p. 1). Such complex solutions allow for the identification of locations critical for climate change, regardless of whether they are located in natural areas or in city centers. The systemic orientation of such a solution, supported by the assumptions of artificial intelligence, will contribute to aspects of climate change monitoring from the perspective of various thematic areas. Geospatial intelligence is a solution with such potential that decision-makers should look for funds to implement it. GeoAI-based network coverage for monitoring systems accelerates capabilities and expands the spectrum of practical applications. Thus, cyberspace is created, focused on the location of places where hazards affecting climate change can occur, often related to natural and weather phenomena.

8.6 Conclusions

In order to be able to stimulate positive climate change, it is necessary to be open to the search for carriers of intelligent climate values, understand them and be able to apply them in organizational—management, technological and economic—financial dimensions. Technological, organizational, process and design innovations can serve this purpose and, supported by wise management, can bring benefits to various groups of actors of socio-economic ecosystems. This approach, which develops into dynamic decision-making processes at the strategic and tactical–operational level, can be an accelerator for the development and growth of a climate-positive economy.

References

Antikainen, M., & Valkokari, K. (2016). A framework for sustainable circular business model innovation. *Technology Innovation Management Review, 6*(7), 5–12. https://doi.org/10.22215/timreview/1000

Bayomi, N., & Fernandez, J. E. (2023). Eyes in the sky: Drones applications in the built environment under climate change challenges. *Drones, 7*(637), 1.

Bekmurzaeva, R., Kalimullin, R., & Aguzarova, F. (2024). Application of drones and artificial intelligence to monitor and protect natural ecosystems. *BIO Web of Conferences, 140*(01008), 1.

Beuren, F. H., Ferreira, M. G. G., & Miguel, P. A. C. (2013). Product-service systems: A literature review on integrated products and services. *Journal of Cleaner Production, 47*, 222–231. https://doi.org/10.1016/j.jclepro.2012.12.028

Bianchini, S., Müller, M., & Pelletier, P. (2022). Artificial intelligence in science: An emerging general method of invention. *Research Policy, 51*, 1.

Bindeeba, D. S., Tukamushaba, E. K., & Bakashaba, R. (2025). Digital transformation and its multidimensional impact on sustainable business performance: Evidence from a meta-analytic review. *Future Business Journal, 11*, 90. https://doi.org/10.1186/s43093-025-00511-z

Bocken, N. M. P., de Pauw, I., Bakker, C., & van der Grinten, B. (2016). Product design and business model strategies for a circular economy. *Journal of Industrial and Production Engineering, 33*(5), 308–320. https://doi.org/10.1080/21681015.2016.1172124

Bocken, N. M. P., Schuit, C. S. C., & Kraaijenhagen, C. (2018). Experimenting with a circular business model: Lessons from eight cases. *Environmental Innovation and Societal Transitions, 28*, 79–95. https://doi.org/10.1016/j.eist.2018.02.001

Boutayeb, A., Lahsen-cherif, I., & El Khadimi, A. (2024, December 17). A comprehensive GeoAI review: Progress, challenges and outlooks. Institut National des Postes et T´el´ecommunications (INPT), 1.

Bencsik, B. (2023). Business models for digital sustainability: Framework development and typology. *Technological Forecasting and Social Change, 187*, Article 122129. https://doi.org/10.1016/j.techfore.2023.122129

Chen, Y., & Zhao, C. (2022). Review of energy sharing: Business models, mechanisms and designs. *IET Renewable Power Generation, 16*(14), 2897–2913. https://doi.org/10.1049/rpg2.12438

Das, S., Sun, Q. (Chayn), & Zhou, H. (2022). GeoAI to implement an individual tree inventory: Framework and application of heat mitigation. *Urban Forestry & Urban Greening, 74*, 1.

Díaz-Delgado, R., Ónodi, G., Kröel-Dulay, G., & Kertész, M. (2019). Enhancement of ecological field experimental research by means of UAV Multispectral Sensing. *Drones, 3*(1)7, 64.

Dowell, M., Lecomte, P., Husband, R., Schulz, J., Mohr, T., Tahara, Y., Eckman, R., Lindstrom, E., Wooldridge, C., Hilding, S., Bates, J., Ryan, B., Lafeuille, J., & Bojinski, S. (2013). Strategy towards an architecture for climate monitoring from space. p. 26. This report is : www.ceos.org; www.wmo.int/sat; http://www.cgms-info.org/

Ferasso, M., Beliaeva, T., Kraus, S., Clauss, T., & Ribeiro-Soriano, D. (2020). Circular economy business models: The state of research and avenues ahead. *Business Strategy and the Environment, 29*(8), 3006–3024. https://doi.org/10.1002/bse.2554

Gleisner, H., Ringer, M. A., & Healy, S. B. (2022). Monitoring global climate change using GNSS radio Occultation. *Climate and Atmospheric Science, 5*(1), 1.

Guandalini, I. (2022). Sustainability through digital transformation: A systematic review. *Journal of Business Research, 142*, 1–17. https://doi.org/10.1016/j.jbusres.2022.01.008

Gupta, A., Nath Dwivedi D., & Kumar Maurya S. (2022). Climate change monitoring using remote sensing, deep learning, and computer vision. *Webology (ISSN: 1735–188X), 19*(2), 3599.

Innovation and Adaptation in the Climate Crisis: Technology for the New Normal Insight Report January 2024. *World Economic Forum*, 2.

Knight, R. (2022). Environmental monitoring: Drones provide critical insights on the impact of climate change. *Climate Science and Research*, 8.

Li, X. (2023). Research on the mechanism of sustainable business model innovation based on digital platform ecosystem. *Technological Forecasting and Social Change, 186*, 122158. https://www.sciencedirect.com/science/article/abs/pii/S0923474823000085

López, F. J. D., Bastein, T., & Tukker, A. (2019). Business model innovation for resource-efficiency, circularity and sustainability: A review. *Ecological Economics, 155*, 20–35. https://doi.org/10.1016/j.ecolecon.2018.03.009

Mishra, S., & Tripathi, A. R. (2021). AI business model: An integrative business approach. *Journal of Innovation and Entrepreneurship, 10*(18), 1.

Murphy, K. (2023). The role of satellites in climate monitoring: A critical tool for studying climate change, weather patterns, and environmental phenomena. *Journal of Space Exploration, 12*(3), 1.

Nussholz, J. (2024). Circular business models for digital technologies in the built environment. In *Circular business models for digital technologies* (pp. 215–228). Springer. https://link.springer.com/chapter/10.1007/978-3-031-39675-5_14

Omali, T. U. (2022). Monitoring climate change using satellite-observed earth's surface temperature: A review. *International Journal of Scientific Research in Physics and Applied Sciences, 10*(4), 15–22, 15.

Shang, T., Zhang, K., Liu, P., & Chen, Z. (2017). A review of energy performance contracting business models: Status and recommendations. *Sustainable Cities and Society, 34*, 203–210. https://doi.org/10.1016/j.scs.2017.06.018

Vezzoli, C., Ceschin, F., Diehl, J. C., & Kohtala, C. (2015). New design challenges to widely implement "sustainable product–service systems." *Journal of Cleaner Production, 97*, 1–12. https://doi.org/10.1016/j.jclepro.2015.02.061

Vikas, V., Sharma, V., Sharma, C., & Singh, A. (2019). Drone technology as a tool to manage climate change. In *Vth J&K Agriculture Science Congress, Climate Change Management for Sustainable Agriculture, Livestock Farming and Ecological Development, SKUAST JAMMU, 14–16* (p. 74).

Weber, M., Beutter, M., Weking, J., Bohm, M., & Krcmar, H. (2022). AI startup business models key characteristics and directions for entrepreneurship research. *Business and Information Systems Engineering, 64*(1), 98.

Yang, J., Gong, P., Fu, R., Zhang, M., Chen, J., Liang, S., Xu, B., Shi, J., & Dickinson, R. (2013). The role of satellite remote sensing in climate change studies. *Nature Climate Change, 3*(10), 875–883.

CHAPTER 9

Climate-Friendly Digital Business Models

Abstract The aim of this chapter is to present climate-friendly digital business models. In order to be able to achieve acceptable results in the area of positive climate change, it is necessary to have an appropriate toolbox. Undoubtedly, at the strategic level, the concept of business models will apply here. Business models offer the opportunity to shape reality through their applicable architecture, which, properly constructed and aggregated in a coherent way, can create even improbable opportunities and benefits. In the case of climate change, it can be a platform for strategic change not only of the processes of strategic thinking about the climate, but above all, for reversing the negative shape and image of many economies of the world while maintaining their economic parameters. From this perspective, climate-friendly digital business models open a new and previously underused space for climate-based development and growth.

Keywords Climate-friendly digital business models · Positive climate change · Opportunities and benefits · Climate-based development and growth

A. Jabłoński and M. Jabłoński, *Digital Business Models and Environmental Action*,
https://doi.org/10.1007/978-3-032-15298-5_9

9.1 Introduction

In order to be able to achieve acceptable results in the area of positive climate change, it is necessary to have an appropriate toolbox. Undoubtedly, at the strategic level, the concept of business models will apply here.

Business models offer the opportunity to shape reality through their applicable architecture, which, properly constructed and aggregated in a coherent way, can create even improbable opportunities and benefits. In the case of climate change, it can be a platform for strategic change not only of the processes of strategic thinking about the climate, but above all, for reversing the negative shape and image of many economies of the world while maintaining their economic parameters. From this perspective, climate-friendly digital business models open a new and previously underused space for climate-based development and growth.

9.2 Climate Business Models

The digital transformation is one of the main catalysts for the green transformation. Digitalization makes it possible to make a climate civilization leap in all areas of human existence. Building and implementing climate business models from the perspective of climate problems in a destructive way affecting the economy, business and society is essential to shaping positive climate change.

Strategic areas that can determine the construction of such business models include the following:

1. The principles of green digitalization

Green digitalization, in this case, is understood as all manifestations of activity embedded in digital solutions that limit, neutralize or create positive climate change. Anything that can be done digitally and does not have an adverse impact on the environment and/or climate will have the potential for green digitalization. This includes, for example, reducing transport through the design and deployment of intelligent transport systems (ITS), developing mobility applications and optimizing delivery routes with the use of artificial intelligence and developing smart energy systems, e.g., smart grids or IoT implementation in buildings. This also applies to the reduction of the IT carbon footprint and RES-based cloud computing, as well as the optimization of energy consumption in data centers and the construction of software for calculating and reporting the carbon footprint.

2. Renewable energy and energy efficiency mechanisms

Energy efficiency can be achieved, among others, by forecasting RES production by means of AI, using digital twins of wind and solar farms, building smart grids, creating virtual power plants (VPP) or using smart metering solutions. Moreover, it is worth paying attention to the construction of intelligent LED lighting systems and intelligent building management systems (BMS).

3. Circular economy principles

The core principles of the circular economy in climate terms include the concept of designing to reduce waste and emissions, keeping products and materials in use for as long as possible, regenerating natural systems, replacing fossil fuels with renewable resources, sharing resources and building closed loops in value chains.

4. The principles of offsetting and climate neutrality

These principles are particularly aimed at building emission measurement and reporting systems, reducing emissions at source, offsetting emissions that cannot be eliminated and implementing solutions for the long-term removal of CO_2 from the atmosphere.

These strategic areas can function together and separately to create new innovative business models, new products and new climate-friendly services.

9.3 Climate-Friendly Digital Business Models

Business models often have a universal and interdisciplinary dimension. This occurs while combining the principles of the digital transformation with those of the climate transformation. As a result of such synergy, symmetry and symbiosis, climate-friendly digital business models can be designed and implemented. They can be defined as business models that

Table 9.1 Selected proposals for climate-friendly digital business models

Type of a business model	*Description*	*Literature sources*
Circular economy business models	Platforms and applications for sharing, reusing and trading second-hand goods, which limits the production of new goods	Antikainen, M., & Valkokari, K. (2016). A framework for sustainable circular business model innovation. Technology Innovation Management Review, 6(7), 5–12. https://doi.org/10.22215/timreview/1000, Bocken, N. M. P., de Pauw, I., Bakker, C., & van der Grinten, B. (2016). Product design and business model strategies for a circular economy. Journal of Industrial and Production Engineering, 33(5), 308–320 https://doi.org/10.1080/21681015.2016.1172124, Bocken, N. M. P., Schuit, C. S. C., & Kraaijenhagen, C. (2018). Experimenting with a circular business model: Lessons from eight cases. Environmental Innovation and Societal Transitions, 28, 79–95. https://doi.org/10.1016/j.eist.2018.02.001, Ferasso, M., Beliaeva, T., Kraus, S., Clauss, T., & Ribeiro-Soriano, D. (2020). Circular economy business models: The state of research and avenues ahead. Business Strategy and the Environment, 29(8), 3006–3024. https://doi.org/10.1002/bse.2554, Chen, Y., & Zhao, C. (2022). Review of energy sharing: Business models, mechanisms and designs. IET Renewable Power Generation, 16(14), 2897–2913, https://doi.org/10.1049/rpg2.12438, Shang, T., et al. (2017). A review of energy performance contracting business models: Status and recommendations. Sustainable Cities and Society, 34, 203–210, https://doi.org/10.1016/j.scs.2017.06.018, López, F. J. D., Bastein, T., & Tukker, A. (2019). Business model innovation for resource-efficiency, circularity and sustainability: A review. Ecological Economics, 155, 20–35, https://doi.org/10.1016/j.ecolecon.2018.03.009., Beuren, F. H., Ferreira, M. G. G., & Miguel, P. A. C. (2013). Product-service systems: A literature review on integrated products and services. Journal of Cleaner Production, 47, 222–231. https://doi.org/10.1016/j.jclepro.2012.12.028, Vezzoli, C., Ceschin, F., Diehl, J. C., & Kohtala, C. (2015). New design challenges to widely implement "sustainable product–service systems." Journal of Cleaner Production, 97, 1–12. https://doi.org/10.1016/j.jclepro.2015.02.061, Bindeeba, D. S., et al. (2025). Digital transformation and its multidimensional impact on sustainable business performance: Evidence from a meta-analytic review. Future Business Journal, 11, 90. https://doi.org/10.1186/s43093-025–00,511-z, Guandalini, I., et al. (2022). Sustainability through digital transformation: A systematic review. Journal of Business Research, 142, 1–17. https://doi.org/10.1016/j.jbusres.2022.01.008, Bencsik, B. (2023). Business models for digital sustainability: Framework development and typology. Technological Forecasting and Social Change, 187, 122,129. https://doi.org/10.1016/j.techfore.2023.122129, Li, X. (2023). Research on the mechanism of sustainable business model innovation based on digital platform ecosystem. Technological Forecasting and Social Change, 186, 122,158. https://www.sciencedirect.com/science/article/abs/pii/S0923474823000085, Nussholz, J. (2024). Circular business models for digital technologies in the built environment. In Circular Business Models for Digital Technologies (pp. 215–228). Springer. https://link.springer.com/chapter/10.1007/978-3-031-39675-5_14
Business models focused on energy efficiency and resource management	The use of digital twins, IoT and smart metering, i.e., a smart metering system to reduce energy, water and material consumption	
Business models based on the Product-as-a-Service concept	Selling access to functionality instead of having a product; digitally monitored, maintained and repaired products, which extends their life cycle	
Business models based on the principles of sustainable digital transformation	Moving services to the RES-powered cloud, digitalization of work (videoconferencing, remote collaboration) reducing travel and emissions	
Business models as platforms supporting pro-ecological decisions	Applications and algorithms for tracking the carbon footprint, optimizing transport and logistics, supporting informed consumer choices	

Source Own study

consistently and scalably generate a simultaneous and combined value proposition that is both an intelligent climate value and an innovative digital value. The result of this generated value is a positive climate impact together with the generated value useful to customers in the form of expected, price-acceptable products and/or services based on the income generation logic in the form of a reasonable profit generated.

Table 9.1 presents selected proposals for climate-friendly digital business models.

The climate-friendly digital business models outlined above show how much can be achieved by generating synergies between different areas of scientific and practical exploration in an interdisciplinary approach of combining common values. The essence of these values materializes in new value propositions and their direct recipients are a wide range of stakeholders.

9.4 Conclusions

Business models, their unique value proposition and their appropriate income generation logic can be focused on climate criteria. If these criteria are a dynamizing factor of these business models and provide a platform for building their configuration, a unique constellation of value delivery focused on reversing adverse climate change in the world will be created. This process can result in the creation of a unique smart climate value for society as a whole. Shaping the stream of such business models and fostering them through the creation of dedicated and appropriate regulatory and formal–legal systems may provide a stimulus to reverse the negative polarization of the economy, which is currently swiftly destroying the climate potential of the world.

CHAPTER 10

The Authors' Original Concept of the Technological Maturity of Companies for the Neutralization of Climate Change

Abstract The aim of this chapter is to present the authors' original concept of the technological maturity of companies for the neutralization of climate change. The technological maturity of companies significantly affects the ability to create solutions that are sufficiently effective to have an impact that ensures the neutralization of climate change. The technological maturity of a company depends on the maturity of its business model. In this context, this maturity is considered in terms of providing specific features intended to create a business model configuration in the present and in the future that will ensure that the company, through its products or services or processes, will have a positive impact on climate change.

Keywords Authors' original concept · Technological maturity of companies · Neutralization of climate change · Maturity of business model

The technological maturity of companies significantly affects the ability to create solutions that are sufficiently effective to have an impact that ensures the neutralization of climate change. The technological maturity of a company depends on the maturity of its business model. In

A. Jabłoński and M. Jabłoński, *Digital Business Models and Environmental Action*,
https://doi.org/10.1007/978-3-032-15298-5_10

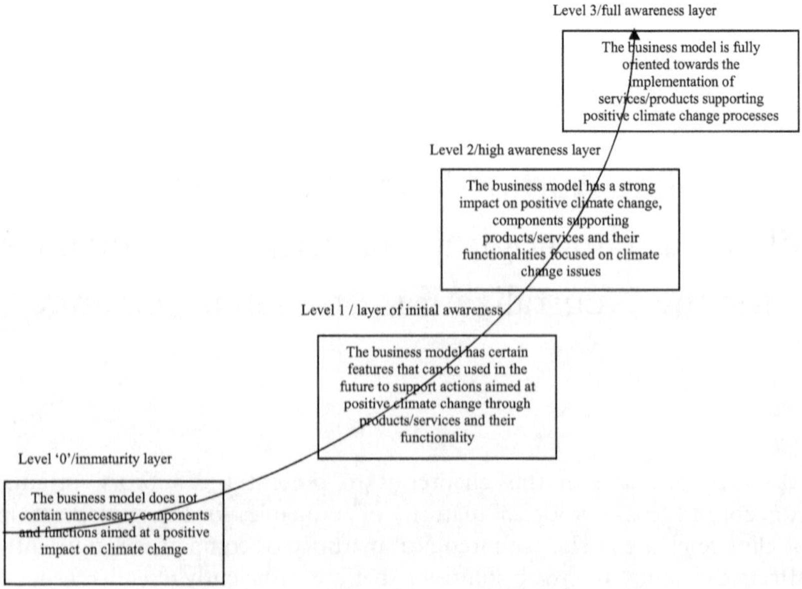

Fig. 10.1 Technological maturity curve of the business models of companies for climate change neutralization (*Source* Own study)

this context, this maturity is considered in terms of providing specific features intended to create a business model configuration in the present and in the future that will ensure that the company, through its products or services or processes, will have a positive impact on climate change. Figure 10.1 shows the process of creating the technological maturity curve of business models for climate change neutralization.

The process proceeds over time from business models mapped to a layer of technological immaturity in the context of climate change determinants without any components or functions focused on a positive impact on climate change. By adding components that create an increasing positive impact on the climate, a higher level of technological maturity of business models is reached. Regardless of its analog or digital form, the mature business model is based on high-awareness assumptions, conducive to the provision of services or products supporting processes with a positive impact on climate change. The process of increasing the technological maturity of business models in the context of climate change runs through four levels from '0' to '3' and is linear, where managers should work intensively to move from lower to higher levels as they become increasingly aware of the impact of business activities on climate change. The presented scheme of action can be a determinant of development and growth strategies of companies aiming for a positive impact on climate change.

CHAPTER 11

The Authors' Original Concept of the Climate Ambidexterity of Companies

Abstract The aim of this chapter is to present the authors' original concept of the climate ambidexterity of companies. The ambidexterity of companes is understood as the ability to simultaneously maintain effectiveness and efficiency in the field of operational activity and ensure the simultaneous ability to create innovative solutions that change the rules of the market game, i.e., game changers, including by using experiments. In this respect, the assumptions of strategic management schools are combined mainly with the resource approach and the positional approach. For the purpose of creating a solution for the climate ambidexterity of companies, ambidexterity assumptions were defined based on an individualized approach to understanding the resource approach and the positional approach in this respect.

Keywords Authors' original concept · Climate ambidexterity of companies · Effectiveness and efficiency · Experiments

The ambidexterity of companies is understood as the ability to simultaneously maintain effectiveness and efficiency in the field of operational activity and ensure the simultaneous ability to create innovative solutions that change the rules of the market game, i.e., game changers,

A. Jabłoński and M. Jabłoński, *Digital Business Models and Environmental Action*,
https://doi.org/10.1007/978-3-032-15298-5_11

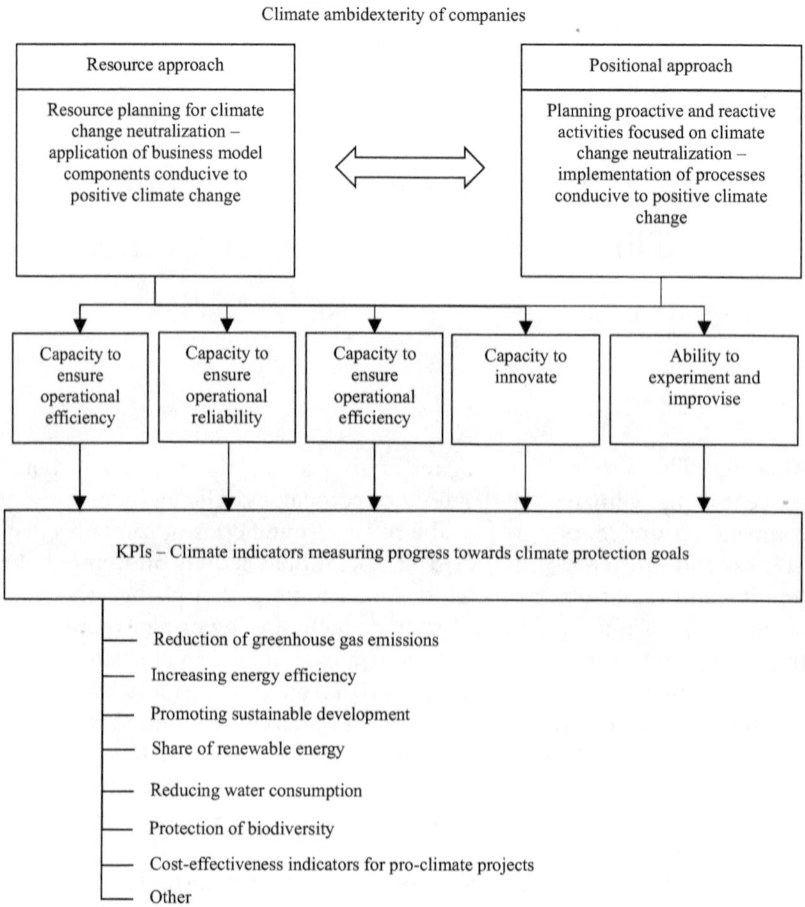

Fig. 11.1 Model of climate ambidexterity of companies (*Source* Own study)

including by using experiments. In this respect, the assumptions of strategic management schools are combined mainly with the resource approach and the positional approach. For the purpose of creating a solution for the climate ambidexterity of companies, ambidexterity assumptions were defined based on an individualized approach to understanding the resource approach and the positional approach in this respect, as presented in Fig. 11.1.

Five core capabilities have been identified from the assumptions adopted for the purpose of climate ambidexterity of companies, which create their strategic behavior, including:

- the capacity to ensure operational efficiency;
- the capacity to ensure operational reliability;
- the capacity to ensure operational efficiency;
- the capacity to innovate;
- the capacity to experiment and improvise.

These capabilities, partly based on a resource-based approach and partly on a positional school of strategic management, are used to create key indicators for achieving KPIs, which are focused on processes for monitoring activities demonstrating progress towards climate protection goals against negative changes. Their number may change compared to the examples of KPIs in the above figure and be adjusted depending on the sector, the scope of activity, scale or size of companies. The presented model of the climate ambidexterity of companies should support the potential created by the adopted business model of companies with a strong positivist orientation for climate change, often based on technological maturity in this field of business models.

CHAPTER 12

The Authors' Original Concept of a Digital Business Model Canvas That Has a Positive Impact on the Neutralization of Climate Change

Abstract The aim of this chapter is to present the authors' original concept of a digital business model canvas that has a positive impact on the neutralization of climate change. It is not easy to search for examples of digital business models focused on a Positive impact on climate change. It is easier to identify business models that support the adverse impact on environmental protection, but the impact on climate change is no longer so obvious. Based on market observations in the field of trends in the design of digital platforms, including those where the climate change aspect is a carrier of development and growth, the authors' original concept of a digital business model canvas positively affecting the neutralization of climate change.

Keywords Authors' original concept · Digital business model canvas · Positive impact · Neutralization of climate change

A. Jabłoński and M. Jabłoński, *Digital Business Models and Environmental Action*,
https://doi.org/10.1007/978-3-032-15298-5_12

It is not easy to search for examples of digital business models focused on a positive impact on climate change. It is easier to identify business models that support the adverse impact on environmental protection, but the impact on climate change is no longer so obvious. Based on market observations in the field of trends in the design of digital platforms, including those where the climate change aspect is a carrier of development and growth, the authors' original concept of a digital business model canvas positively affecting the neutralization of climate change presented in Table 12.1 was developed.

The designed canvas of the digital business model combines knowledge of the function of the purpose of creating this canvas, i.e., creating a form of description of digital business models positively affecting climate change, mainly in relation to the neutralization of these changes, on the one hand, in the context of the dynamics of changes in this field, and on the other hand, based on the experience of the digital transformation of the modern global economy. An additional component in reversing the negative trend of climate change affecting weather anomalies and the destruction of the earth's ecosystem is crucial to the success of modern companies. It is the core carrier of modern success and should be an essential component in the design of modern traditional and digital business models. The digital transformation should therefore support the creation of business ventures that focus on creating an impact that can be identified as reinforcing the reversal of adverse climate change that threatens the current social, political and economic order.

Table 12.1 Modified business model canvas of a digital platform connecting organizations, companies and communities to monitor, reduce and offset CO_2 emissions, including a component of actions to reverse climate change processes at the company level

Key partners	*Key actions*	*Value proposition*	*Customer relations*	*Customer segments*
– Technology companies (IoT, cloud, AI) – Financial institutions (green investments, coal loans) – Environmental organizations and local governments – Universities and research institutes	–Support in the implementation of the net-zero strategy thanks to the integration of data with IoT, AI and blockchain –Customer carbon footprint analysis –Verification and certification of offset projects –Education and support of clients in pro-climate activities	–Transparent tracking of the effects of reduction and compensation activities in real time –Tools for personalized carbon footprint reduction plans for companies and local governments –Marketplace of certified offset projects (e.g., afforestation, RES, soil remediation)	–Self-service platform with personalization –Online expert support (chat, video consultations) –A community of users and a forum for exchanging experiences –Gamification of emission reduction processes (badges, rankings)	–Local governments pursuing local strategies for adaptation to climate change –NGOs and environmental organizations –Individual consumers who are environmentally conscious and want to neutralize their carbon footprint
	Key resources		**Distribution channels**	

(continued)

Table 12.1 (continued)

Key partners	*Key actions*	*Value proposition*	*Customer relations*	*Customer segments*
	–Integration system with IoT and emission bases –Partners certifying offset projects –A team of programmers, data analysts and climate experts –Development and maintenance of the SaaS platform –Integration of data from various sources (IoT, ERP, satellites)		–Mobile and web application (a SaaS platform) –API integration with ERP, CRM, and IoT systems –Webinars and online training –Social media and educational campaigns –Partnerships with industry organizations and financial institutions	
Cost structure –Costs of cloud and cybersecurity –Marketing and customer acquisition –Salaries of a team of experts and programmers –Audits and certification of offset projects			**Structure of revenue** –SaaS subscription (different levels of functionality) –Commissions on transactions in the offset projects marketplace –Fees for ESG reports and emission reduction certificates –Premium consulting services –Sales of aggregated (anonymous) data to research and market institutions	
Key distinguishing factors of the business model: –The use of Blockchain technology for full transparency of tracking emission reductions –Applying AI to predict and recommend optimal climate action				

<table>
<tr><th>Key partners</th><th>Key actions</th><th>Value proposition</th><th>Customer relations</th><th>Customer segments</th></tr>
<tr><td colspan="5">–The of use of IoT for real-time measurement (e.g., air quality sensors, energy consumption monitoring)
–The sharing economy—the possibility for small actors to join forces in large-scale neutralization projects
Impact on climate change:
–An attitude based on trying to reverse climate change at the company level
–Building employee awareness for climate change risk neutralization
–Creating pro-climate innovations
–Pro-climate attitudes in everyday work and private life
–Learning the processes of reversing the adverse impact on the climate
–Visible leadership of top management towards pro-climate behavior
–The use of game changer technologies and innovations that contribute to positive climate change
–Integration of climate change monitoring services into normal operational processes—implementation of climate change monitoring systems at the company level
–Investment in modern technologies and technological progress—an obsession with the climate
–Application of the principle: 'Reasonable profit today—climate impact tomorrow'
–Application of climate responsibility assumptions
–Treating the business ecosystem as a socio-technical system
–Being positively oriented towards the joyful conduct of business based on satisfaction that something good is being done for the close and distant environment, as a consequence for future generations</td></tr>
</table>

Source Own study

CHAPTER 13

Development of a Set of Axioms for Harnessing the Potential of the Technological Revolution to Address Climate Change

Abstract The content presented in this monograph is aimed at proving the following hypotheses put forward by the authors:

Hypothesis 1: The technological revolution strengthens the fight against climate change through environmental action.
Hypothesis 2: The functions of digital business models influence the fight against climate change.

Testing both of these hypotheses, through analytical studies, literature studies and syntheses included in individual chapters, led to the conclusion that both hypotheses are falsifiable. The technological revolution significantly affects the creation of solutions to neutralize climate change, which is noted by the growing budgets of the European Union, international organizations, states, regions and enterprises for this purpose. At the company level, the trend of implementing new and innovative strategies is clearly marked, as well as shaping digital business models to fit through their functions to create positive changes in the face of worrying climate anomalies. The world of a growing economy must be based on climate-smart technologies. Strategies to date for the use

A. Jabłoński and M. Jabłoński, *Digital Business Models and Environmental Action*,
https://doi.org/10.1007/978-3-032-15298-5_13

of natural resources adversely affecting indicators determining adverse climate change are slowly shifting to a role supporting modern technologies of energy production.

Keywords Development of a set of axioms · Harnessing the potential of the technological revolution · Climate change · Digital business models

The content presented in this monograph is aimed at proving the following hypotheses put forward by the authors:

> Hypothesis 1: The technological revolution strengthens the fight against climate change through environmental action.
> Hypothesis 2: The functions of digital business models influence the fight against climate change.

Testing both of these hypotheses, through analytical studies, literature studies and syntheses included in individual chapters, led to the conclusion that both hypotheses are falsifiable. The technological revolution significantly affects the creation of solutions to neutralize climate change, which is noted by the growing budgets of the European Union, international organizations, states, regions and enterprises for this purpose. At the company level, the trend of implementing new and innovative strategies is clearly marked, as well as shaping digital business models to fit through their functions to create positive changes in the face of worrying climate anomalies. The world of a growing economy must be based on climate-smart technologies. Strategies to date for the use of natural resources adversely affecting indicators determining adverse climate change are slowly shifting to a role supporting modern technologies of energy production. Three key types of energy are crucial in this regard. Energy is a key indicator of prosperity, but its cost to both the producer and the environment should be as low as possible. Therefore, modern efforts are aimed at searching for cheap sources of energy and improving its availability. Unfortunately, the wealth of nations, including their prosperity, is strongly associated with energy consumption and, consequently, with negative carbon dioxide emissions, which affects climate change, manifested by numerous weather anomalies and anomalies visible in the world of nature and the management of natural resources. Since the combustion of fossil fuels consists of their oxidation, the result of this process is carbon dioxide emissions. Therefore, in the world of science, industry and business, intensive work is currently being carried out in the form of scientific projects related to practice aimed at searching for progressive solutions that change the conditions of the game, so-called game changers aimed at creating innovative solutions that are part of the global and systemic trend of the digital, energy and climate transformation. All these solutions, in order to achieve a noticeable impact for our planet, must be implemented at all levels of human activity, both in the fields of industry and business and in the direct behavior of individuals. Therefore, the most important thing is the awareness and belief in the reversibility of current processes that destroy the Earth's ecosystem and the living environment of people. It is therefore necessary to improve energy efficiency, change energy sources to those that have a neutral impact on the climate, but in particular to design new business models that have a positive impact on climate change in the sense that they work to reverse this negative trend. Naturally, the scale of change can be counted in decades, but business has always been ahead of the effects, which have been repeatedly evaluated over the years. The principle of ***'reasonable profit today – climate impact tomorrow'*** is important. Such an approach requires the search for balance between business wealth, energy policy and carbon emissions. Such assumptions must be adopted by the creators of new technologies on the basis of which they want to create socially acceptable, innovative and sustainable business models. A society that has hitherto focused on consumption should now accept a new understanding of the well-being of life based on values, trust and respect for the nature of the earth. It can even be said that consumption in the 1980s–1990s is now 'passe.' The lifestyle predominantly associated with Scandinavian countries is preferred, along with maintaining proximity to nature. The new economy, new business and newly climate-conscious people expect a technological revolution to reverse adverse climate change. This is in the interest of the whole world, not just a small group of climate activists. The limits of the growth of global consumption have long been exceeded; therefore, the concepts, models and solutions presented in the monograph should be positively accepted by readers as a way to change the approach to life and create new space for shaping pro-climate attitudes.

The research, its results, analyses and content in the monograph underlie the formulation of the following set of axioms proving the importance of the subject and indicating where strategic and operational activities should be directed at the levels of regions, cities and companies:

1. Business management in the context of digital transformation faces huge challenges, where the current paradigms, solutions and theoretical foundations of decision-making are undergoing significant changes.
2. Revolutionary solutions in the processes of designing business models based on digital platforms, the technology mergers of key providers of innovative solutions taking into account the implementation of socio-technical systems are factors influencing the needs of change.
3. As the world is not equal in terms of the same standard of technological progress, sustainable solutions must be sought to ensure the success of all regions of the world.
4. The digital revolution is based on the assumptions of creative destruction, which leads to opportunities to create new business models that take into account new management rules resulting from technological progress. Factors generating revolutionary solutions are extracted from the external and internal environment.
5. The modern technological revolution should be focused on neutralizing the risks associated with the adverse impact of industry on climate change and be innovative enough to influence change effectively—to reverse negative phenomena.
6. The changes of recent years in the world indicate that the boundary between the physical and digital worlds is becoming increasingly blurred.
7. Technological and industrial systems based on automation, robotization, artificial intelligence and technical diagnostics determine the mechanisms of the dynamically progressing technological revolution in the modern world.
8. Action-oriented products and services supporting environmental processes, and predictive systems for capturing anomalies and weather dysfunctions and negative changes in the natural ecosystem and climate, are core factors underpinning digital business models.
9. Digital platforms, along with their functions and achievements in the sphere of social impact, are part of the strategy of creating high energy efficiency, promoting the use of solar energy and wind

energy; in general, renewable energy sources. They influence the creation of business models based on carbon capture technologies, building solutions based on bioenergy, creating zero-emission energy sources, monitoring and reducing carbon emissions.

10. Digital climate services are developing dynamically due to the needs arising from public concern about weather changes, anomalies and dysfunctions of natural systems. Negative weather and climate trends force us to search for solutions mainly based on predictive solutions for capturing potential events before they occur.
11. The model of climate adaptation has the character of a dynamic stratified system, where changes pass from above to lower levels of social life functioning. Change processes are cascaded from the level of the world affected by space to regions, cities and even businesses. Thus, the system is fully airtight and affects all areas of social life in the world.
12. Combining the needs for the implementation of climate services, understood as actions aimed at detecting and responding to potential trends of change through a system of alerts or actions reducing the risk of negative scenarios in this area, the need arises to seek the possibility of predicting changes. Therefore, simulating various weather anomalies or climate changes in this natural area is possible only through the use of digital economy solutions.
13. The reconfiguration of the value chain towards the circular economy can help boost the growth of technology-based companies. This approach fits into the contemporary paradigm of creating value through the use of revolutionary technologies, especially in the area of environmental protection, climate change monitoring services and the adaptation of business solutions to the expectations of the broadly understood society.
14. Climate knowledge management is a very important component in shaping and developing climate responsibility. This applies to organizational, managerial and technological knowledge. Climate knowledge management should serve to develop climate capital within the organization both at the level of individuals, i.e., personnel of the organization, and at the institutional level, i.e., the entire organization.
15. The climate resistance and resilience of a region, cities or companies are core concepts that classify the key challenges of climate

change. Climate resistance is the ability to protect against dynamic climate change. Climate resilience can be defined as the ability to maintain comprehensive climate protection while ensuring the capacity for sustainable development at the level of various existential factors conditioned by the specific operating criteria of a region, a city or a company.

16. Climate responsibility should be based on reliable scientific results—scientific evidence. There are numerous theories denying science in favor of pseudoscience, rubbish, nonsense, description of miracles and common nonsense functioning in public space. Science should not give in to questioning the basic facts and should fight for the truth.
17. Technological progress caused by innovation is changing the rules of the game in the space of life and business. Creative destruction is essential in areas related to environmental protection, including climate change issues.
18. Solutions to halt adverse climate change are related in particular to the digital transformation, the greening of business processes, the development of new forms of energy generation and inventiveness, especially in the area of artificial intelligence.
19. Extensive information networks are essential for modern climate change monitoring. A network effect built with complex monitoring systems distributed in such a way as to ensure the best possible measurement capacity is necessary. Artificial intelligence solutions play a particular role in this regard. The ability to improve climate change monitoring systems is a prerequisite for better analysis of the factors responsible for the state of the climate.
20. Building and implementing climate business models from the perspective of climate problems affecting the economy, business and society in a disruptive way are crucial to shaping positive climate change.
21. By adding components to the configuration of business models that have an increasingly positive impact on the climate, a higher level of technological maturity of business models is achieved. Regardless of whether they have a stronger traditional or digital nature, the most mature business model is based on high-awareness assumptions and is fully focused on the implementation of services or products supporting the processes of positive impact on climate change through the company's activities.

22. The model of climate ambidexterity of companies favors their strategic behaviors. It is crucial to simultaneously develop numerous different abilities such as the capacity to ensure operational efficiency, operational reliability, operational efficiency, company innovation and the capacity to experiment and improvise.
23. Contemporary descriptions of business models, including in particular digital business models, should contain an additional component on climate change and the role of business models in the process of reversing the adverse impact of climate on human life processes and the nature of the earth.

13.1 Conclusion

The theories, concepts, models, practical solutions and technologies presented in the monograph have been used by the authors to demonstrate the leading role in the processes of neutralization and mitigation of climate change risks played by actions taken by business managers seeking, through plans, strategies and experiments, to shape their business models aimed at reversing the adverse impact resulting from climate change. At the same time, they must not forget the fundamental business objective of creating market value, but they should do so if they want to maintain long-term sustainability and development by complying with the **'reasonable profit today – climate impact tomorrow'** principle. The technological revolution visible through the prism of many activities carried out at the level of regions, cities and companies is conducive to the design of strategies aimed at creating solutions that halt the negative phenomena of climate change. Depleted reserves of fossil fuels, the rising cost of their extraction and the struggle between powers based on the possession thereof releases bad energy and destroys trust and cooperation based on partnership, honesty and respect. Therefore, the change towards the implementation of pro-climate solutions is not only of a business nature, but enters the space of political and social relations as well. All stakeholders should ensure that energy is less macroeconomic and that business decentralization provides a level playing field for all talented individuals to develop their innovative ideas. The ability to use technological progress to neutralize adverse climate change contributes to the creation of new traditional and digital business models. The climate change impact component is becoming increasingly important in their structure and will enable the company to obtain a financial benefit from investment in this positive action focused on neutralizing climate change. This may not only deliver value to shareholders, but in particular to the stakeholders of implemented solutions. Those companies that will build factors influencing the reversal of negative weather and climate anomalies in the canvas of their business model and even create pro-climate services will achieve the best results in the near future. These results will be counted not only through money, but through social acceptance and positive impact, contributing to improving the well-being of people and protecting the land from devastation and over-exploitation. This approach should be the standard in the near future and a new perspective on well-being and respect for one's own land should be a challenge for all of us, as responsible citizens of the world.

Therefore, the following research questions were posed:

1. Can companies with top managers focused on reversing climate change, through their actions, foster processes that reverse climate change?
2. Can modern theories, technologies, concepts, solutions, methods and models serve to neutralize the risk of climate change-based phenomena?
3. Are individual actions against the background of global strategies of large corporations at all noticeable in the wider climate context?
4. Does it make sense to engage in the processes of climate change neutralization in the absence of threats to military, economic, social and migration security and the speed of technological change, which has been staggering in recent years?
5. Can a human being influence climate change by supporting his or her conscious actions in this regard?
6. What technologies and technological and organizational solutions can support the processes of reversing the trend of climate change, which affects weather anomalies and changes in the structure of the functioning of the earth as a planet?

The above questions were answered in the affirmative in the course of research, analysis, studies, analyses and synthesis.

There is certainly a need for further research into the impact of climate change on the functioning of companies and, conversely, the impact of strategic and operational activities of companies on reversing the negative trends of climate change and seeking stability and climate security. What is needed in this respect is to develop pro-climate awareness, knowledge of the processes within the climate processes of the earth and its behavior against the background of human influence on its ecosystem.

As the authors of this monograph, we are aware of numerous limitations in relation to the hypotheses and research questions posed, but we hope that such an interdisciplinary approach to this issue will provoke a lively scientific discussion and will help develop a new perspective of the difficult phenomena that pose a challenge not only to the world of science but to the whole world and the people living in it.

Index

A. Jabłoński and M. Jabłoński, *Digital Business Models and Environmental Action*, https://doi.org/10.1007/978-3-032-15298-5

FSC
www.fsc.org
MIX
Papier | Fördert gute Waldnutzung
FSC® C083411

Kolibri 360 GmbH
Ferdinand-Jühlke-Straße 7
99095 Erfurt, Deutschland
produktsicherheit@kolibri360.de